STEELWORKERS RANK-AND-FILE

STEELWORKERS RANK-AND-FILE

The Political Economy of a Union Reform Movement

Philip W. Nyden

PRAEGER

PRAEGER SPECIAL STUDIES • PRAEGER SCIENTIFIC
BERGIN & GARVEY PUBLISHERS, INC.

Library of Congress Cataloging in Publication Data

Nyden, Philip W.
  Steelworkers rank and file.

  Bibliography: p.
  Includes indexes.
  1. Trade-unions—Iron and steel workers—United States.
  2. United Steelworkers of America. I. Title.
  HD6515.I5N93   1984   331.88'1691'-073   83-22462
  ISBN 0-03-063370-2

Bergin & Garvey Publishers, Inc.
670 Amherst Road
South Hadley, Massachusetts 01075

Published in 1984 by Praeger Publishers
CBS Educational and Professional Publishing
A Division of CBS, Inc.
521 Fifth Avenue, New York, New York 10175 U.S.A.

456789   056   987654321

Printed in the United States of America

59,042

31,8816910973
985

CONTENTS

CONTENTS

ACKNOWLEDGEMENTS

When I have read acknowledgements, I always thought thanks to wives and other family members were given as an afterthought. However, after working on this book, I have come to realize the importance of my family's support and patience. My wife--also a sociologist--accompanied me during many of the interviews and participated in the research process, providing me with valuable insights. I can only measure in weeks the time Gwen spent reading countless drafts of the original dissertation and later the revised manuscript. At the same time, my wife, my three-year old daughter, Johanna, and now my six-month old daughter, Elisabeth, have been patient and have tolerated my weekend absences when I was off writing in my office. Because this family support has been crucial in allowing me to complete this book, I would like to acknowledge it first and foremost. I should add that my brother, Paul--who got me interested in the issue of rank-and-file insurgency in unions--and my parents--who have been instrumental in the development of my career and my interests--are also due acknowledgement. As for others who have played a key role in this project, I first would like generally to recognize the hundreds of rank-and-file activists who have fueled the reform movement in the Steelworkers union. Without them there would have been no insurgency to study. More than once, the people I interviewed expressed incredulity as to the significance of their knowledge. The pages following are testimony that the information they provided was extensive, detailed, and insightful.

There are a few people I especially would like to thank. Jim and Betty Balanoff provided guidance in the initial stages of research. Cec Taylor and Anne Forrest have also enriched my research not only through their observations--particularly their perspective as Canadians--but also through their friendship. My dissertation committee at the University of Pennsylvania--Fred Block, Magali Sarfatti Larson, and Jan Smith--provided guidance. In particular, Fred helped me to moderate the unconscious excesses of a researcher emersed in a political movement and later went a step further than most dissertation advisors by providing extensive advice in changing the dissertation into a publishable manuscript. The administration and faculty of Calumet College in Hammond,

Indiana, where I taught between 1975 and 1979, provided encouragement. More recently, my colleagues in the Sociology-Anthropology Department at Loyola University of Chicago have provided the feedback needed to complete the book. Partial financial support for my research was provided by the Louis M. Rabinowitz Foundation. Dave Gabrovich at the Loyola University computer center provided help in making modifications in the computer programs needed in preparing the final copy for printing. Most importantly, I would like to thank Bergin & Garvey Publishers for making publication possible.

Chapter 1

Rank-and-File Insurgency:
A Theoretical Framework

The ability of internal grassroots reform movements to bring about lasting structural and ideological reforms in American unions has long been the subject of debate. With the rising unrest among rank-and-file union members in the 1970s, trade unionists and social researchers alike have raised questions as to why rank-and-file movements emerge and why they succeed or fail. What are the conditions and issues that precipitate rank-and-file disenchantment? How does disenchantment get translated into a social movement which seeks to bring about union reforms and changes in workplace relations? How do the broader social, economic, and political environments, e.g. the structure of industry, affect the goals and strategies of rank-and-file insurgencies? How does union structure affect reform goals and strategies? In what ways do the goals and strategies of the rank-and-file movement itself affect the probability that it will be successful in bringing about lasting changes in union policy? In the 1980s, with the decline of basic manufacturing industries and the drop in union membership, new questions about the future of reform movements and the viability of unions themselves are also being asked.

STEELWORKERS UNION AS A CASE STUDY

I am using the concept of progressive rank-and-file insurgency here to refer to those activities aimed at molding unions into more responsive organizations which will protect workers in all aspects of their relationship with management. The restructured union would work not only to maintain optimal wages--as most unions attempt to do already--but also to increase worker control over job issues on the shopfloor--as most unions today do not seriously attempt to do. Such job issues may include safety, promotion, scheduling and speed of production. Although progressive rank-and-file activity is ultimately aimed at strengthening the worker's position vis-a-vis management, it is also directed at adopting and maintaining organizational structures that will make union leadership more responsive to rank-and-file interests--structures which will also discourage the development of oligarchic leadership.

I have chosen to examine the rank-and-file movement in the United Steelworkers of America (USWA) as a case study of progressive grassroots insurgency, for a number of reasons. The USWA is characteristic of many other industrial unions such as the autoworker, rubber worker, electrical worker, and machinist unions, that were organized or significantly expanded in the 1930s. Like these other unions, the Steelworkers union was organized in the Depression years and has since undergone an organizational maturation process. Since its first years, it has grown in size and has diversified its membership base by organizing workers in other industries and by merging with other smaller unions. Its internal organizational governance--the interrelation of international, regional, and local bodies--is similar to many other unions.* Although some rank-and-file reformers may argue that the top leadership has not been responsive to the membership, little outright corruption has ever been uncovered at top levels of the union. Unlike the well-publicized corruption in unions such as the International Brotherhood of Teamsters, the Laborers' International, and the Hotel Employees and

---

* Many American unions are "International" unions because they represent workers in both the United States and Canada. The districts are geographical regions which may cover anywhere between a part of a metropolitan area to a few states, depending on the number of union members in the area. Locals generally represent workers at a particular plant.

Restaurant Employees International Union, embezzlement, exorbitant leadership salaries, and connections with organized crime have not been prominent characteristics of the Steelworkers union.

Its size also makes the USWA a significant subject for a case study of union behavior. With 1.2 million members in the mid-1970s, it was the largest industrial union in the AFL-CIO. Movements to reform the USWA had the potential of influencing AFL-CIO policy. Whether or not they were successful, grassroots movements in the USWA were clearly of central interest to all American union leaders and union members. In the 1980s, size continues to make the Steelworkers union an important subject for study. However, now it is a change in size--a decline in membership--that is relevant. As has been the case with most other larger American unions--particularly those in manufacturing--the early 1980s has been an era of declining membership. The best estimates of current USWA membership (provided by union leaders) show between 500,000 and 600,000 dues-paying members--a significant drop since the 1970s. This obviously has had and will have an effect on the rank-and-file reform movement in the union.

The Steelworkers was also an obvious choice because of the highly visible level of insurgent activity at local, regional, and international levels of the union in the 1970s. The district- and union-wide campaigns of Edward Sadlowski, which received national coverage, were the tip of the insurgent iceberg. Underlying the Sadlowski campaigns were local and regional insurgent networks which provided the author with a fertile setting in which to study rank-and-file insurgency. Furthermore, the fact that many rank and filers active in the 1970s were also active in earlier insurgencies, provided me with a window through which the earlier history of grassroots activity in the USWA could be observed. Because the rank-and-file movement has been particularly strong among the basic steelworker segment of the USWA (which includes workers from many other industries) the book will concentrate on this portion of the union membership.

Another advantage of selecting the Steelworkers union became apparent only after the research had begun in 1975. The contraction of the steel industry in the late 1970s and early 1980s gave me a valuable opportunity to look at the impact of industrial decline on union organization and the rank-and-file insurgency. The present reduction in USWA rank-and-file activity, after years of ascendency, is valuable in understanding the relationship between a social movement and the broader political economy. It is also useful in understanding the internal weaknesses in the movement--flaws which became apparent only when the movement was subjected to the stress of a declining economy. At the same time, it is helpful in understanding how certain components of the reform movement persevere and modify themselves to stay alive. The local union presidents' rejection of two basic steel "concessions" contracts in the 1982-83 basic steel negotiations is testimony of continued dissidence. The emergence of free "food banks" for laid-off union members as well as the development of community-wide unemployed workers' committees are examples of the rank-and-file movement's attempts to respond to industrial decline in the 1980s. It may be too early to tell what consequences this has for the reform movement or the union itself, but it is apparent that the 1980s will be a period of significant change.

The book is neither a "how-to" book for union insurgents nor a study aimed at falsely raising hopes of present rank-and-file reformers. However, the analysis of the present decline discussed at the end of the book does suggest a number of strategies that the movement may follow in rejuvenating itself. These strategies involve a broadening of labor-community alliances to increase labor's political and economic strength. It is best to leave this discussion until the end of the book. At this point it is useful to outline a brief theoretical framework with which to analyze 40 years of grassroots activity in the union.

THEORETICAL FRAMEWORK

A synthesis of a number of theoretical models will be used in analyzing the character of rank-and-file insurgency. Theories will be drawn from literature by neo-Marxist political economists, sociologists who have studied social movements, and researchers who have closely examined organizational behavior. In constructing a broad map of how social institutions influence and regulate social relations on the job, industrial structure, and union:management relations, neo-Marxist political economists provide particularly valuable insights into the growth and direction of grassroots political movements. At the same time, they provide an understanding of the formidable obstacles facing union reform movements. First let us look at the nature of the reform movement.

Rank-and-File Caucuses and the Reform Movement

The reform movement does not always have the visible leaders, formal organization, active staff, and office space which characterize more stable organizations. Instead one has to think of the reform movement as an omnipresent but loosely bound social grouping which expands and contracts depending on social, economic, and political conditions in the workplace, union, and broader society. Sociologist Roberta Ash Garner captures this view in her definition of a "social movement" as

> a set of actions of a group of people. These actions have the following characteristics: they are self-consciously directed toward changing the social structure and/or ideology of a society, and they either are carried on outside of ideologically

legitimated channels of change or use these channels in innovative ways [Garner 1977:1].

Much of the rank-and-file activity in the USWA fits into this framework because participants have consciously sought to change social structure by changing both internal union power relationships and the relationship between the union and employers. The Steelworker rank-and-file movement also meets the second criterion--carrying on activities outside "legitimate channels" or using the channels in "innovative ways"--in that many of its political activities have been carried on outside of official union channels. The formation of unofficial Steelworker rank-and-file reform caucuses--particularly at the local level--is probably the best example of extra-legitimate activity. These caucuses may start as informal networks of grassroots workers who have gripes about their workplace or union. They may grow into more formal "caucuses" which hold regular meetings, slate candidates in local union elections, publish newsletters, and participate as a group in local union meetings. In addition to formation of caucuses, other extra-legitimate activities have included the use of legal suits in attempting to overturn contract settlements and union elections, as well as solicitation of outside support in insurgent electoral challenges to incumbent union officials. Such modes of operation are usually not accepted as "legitimate" in unions--particularly among union leaders--even though they may appear legitimate in civil politics.

"Social movement" is also a useful concept in the present study because there have been times when the rank-and-file movement has been an amorphous collection of small social networks without any overall formal organizational structure. Although varying degrees of coalition have occurred among both the insurgent networks and some of the more formal local insurgent "caucuses," the level of coordinated activity has had its ups and downs over time. Social movement theories are particularly useful in understanding this sporadic developmental process. The mercurial character of social movements means that social movements have an "ambiguous potential" for achieving specific goals (Garner 1977:204). This is largely due to their amorphous form--particularly at early stages. Herbert Blumer (1955:200) explains that

> General social movements take the form of groping and unco-ordinated efforts. They have only a general direction, toward which they move in a slow, halting, yet persistent fashion. As movements they are unorganized, with neither established leadership nor recognized membership and little guidance and control.... Such a movement is episodic.... Leaders are likely to be "voices in the wilderness," pioneers without any solid following, and frequently not very clear about their own goals.

By recognizing the ambiguity in social movement goals, the presence of limited coordination of activity, and the episodic nature of social movements one becomes aware of the vulnerability of movements to "cooptation" by or "incorporation" into the very structures they seek to change. One also becomes sensitive to the fact that movements are shaped by the organizational environment and dominant political economy in which they function. This is not to say that the political economy *determines* what form and direction a social movement will take. The development of the reform movement has also been influenced by grassroots leaders themselves.

Resource Mobilization and Reform Organizations

One can speak of the existence of a rank-and-file movement in the USWA since its first years, even though no formal organizational embodiment of the movement was apparent. Particular "caucuses" and rank-and-file "organizations" have arisen only from time to time. These organizations are the visible outcroppings of a less apparent movement which always remains below the surface. (The distinction between social movements and social movement organizations is discussed in McCarthy and Zald (1977:1217-18).) More specifically, they are products of the movement's ability to mobilize resources--financial and political support--in the workplace, community, and broader society.

This "resource mobilization" perspective emphasizes the crucial role that grassroots leaders can play in manipulating the social environment to further insurgent political interests. (The "resource mobilization" perspective is discussed further in Zald and McCarthy (1979).) Successful movements and successful leaders are those that find the political routes that circumvent the opposition's blocades and build upon rank-and-file strengths. In their article on resource mobilization by social movements, John McCarthy and Mayer Zald (1977:1213) explain that

> The resource mobilization approach emphasizes both societal support and constraint of social movement phenomena. It examines the variety of resources that must be mobilized, the linkages of social movements to other groups, the dependence of movements upon external support for success, and the tactics used by authorities to control or incorporate movements.... The new approach depends more upon political sociological and economic theories than upon the social psychology of collective behavior.

Emphasis is placed on the grassroots leader's and the organization's role in defining and manipulating disenchantment. McCarthy and Zald argue that "grievances and discontent may be defined, created, and manipulated by issue entrepreneurs and organizations" (1977:1215). Movements are not viewed as emerging "naturally" or developing without direction. Rather they are viewed as products of conscious action on the part of leaders and members. Therefore, while organizational contexts and the broader political economy do place constraints on movement development--or are at least likely to affect the character of the movement--the resource mobilization perspective suggests that the conscious choices made by social movement leaders and members in selecting strategies and organizational forms are crucial to movement success and failure. Thus, in understanding the evolution of the Steelworkers rank-and-file movement, one should look not only at environment as constraining movement development, but also at the movement leadership's choice of structures and strategies.

A CAPITALIST INSTITUTIONAL DOMINANCE MODEL

The "capitalist institutional dominance model" is the description best given to the theoretical perspective used throughout the book. It combines the neo-Marxist view of political economy with elements of other theories. As stated above, the theory is founded on the observation that social relations in the workplace, as well as internal union structures, are strongly influenced by social, political, and economic factors in the whole society. These broader elements change as the society evolves through different stages and the social organization of production changes. The social, political, and economic structures that have emerged in twentieth-century America are integrally related to the development of modern monopoly capitalism.[1]

Generally neo-Marxists argue that the highly centralized and powerful private corporate management of monopoly capitalism relies on a broad range of social institutions, e.g. politics, education, and family, to integrate workers into the workplace social system. Through this integration, management can maintain high levels of labor force productivity and the concomitant high level of profits. According to the neo-Marxist view, union structure and ideology are strongly influenced by capitalist social institutions. In *Job Control and Union Structure*, John Herding argues that a broad understanding of the capitalist political economy is essential to understanding the structure of unions and the behavior of union leaders. Herding (1972:65) writes:

> In terms of formal organization theory--of conflict and adaptation within organizations, of integrating individuals into organizations, and so forth--...the concrete substance of class conflict underlying and directing the particular organizations of labor is overlooked.

Also, social institutions in capitalism maintain an influence over unions and the workplace through both coercion and ideological domination.   Richard Hyman and R. H. Fryer (1977:155) identify two factors:

> First, capital normally has the privileged access to the coercive sanctions of the state.... Second, unequal economic and political power give capital a crucial influence over processes of *ideological formation*: legitimating its own predominance and inhibiting effective challenge on the part of labour.

While the institutional dominance model does describe how the status quo and apparent stability are maintained through social integration and coercion, at the same time, the inevitability of social conflict is assumed.   This helps to explain both the emergence of unions and the subsequent emergence of rank-and-file reform movements.   In *Contested Terrain*, Richard Edwards describes how worker:management conflict is inevitable in a social process where employers are trying to extract labor from workers who "have no direct stake in profits."   The most prominent manifestation of this confict is in the workplace, where

> Conflict arises over how work shall be organized, what work pace shall be established, what conditions producers must labor under, what rights workers shall enjoy and how the various employees of the enterprise shall relate to each other.   The workplace becomes a battleground, as employers attempt to extract the maximum effort from workers and workers necessarily resist their bosses' impositions [1979:13].

It is this conflict that initially gives rise to labor unions.

However, according to the neo-Marxist perspective, unions themselves become one of the institutions of social control.   Confict is "institutionalized," i.e. it is confined to the bargaining table, ameliorated through a grievance system, or managed by government regulation.   In this process of give and take, unions make some gains and employers make others. Monopoly capital retains control over workplace matters that might affect productivity--e.g. speed of production, work hours, hiring, promotions, and safety regulations.   Unions provide a guarantee that corporate productivity standards will be met, e.g. through agreements prohibiting strikes during the life of the contract, establishment of productivity standards, and introduction of standard work hours.   In exchange, monopoly capital makes concessions on economic issues, i.e. wages and benefits.

It is the influence of the capitalist institutions that pressures union leaders to stress economic demands over job control demands.   The neo-Marxists argue that union leaders have an easier time winning economic concessions from management than they do winning more control over workplace decision making because the former do not undermine corporate power or assets. Increased labor costs can be offset by increased prices. On the other hand, inroads in union job control could not be offset as easily. A stronger union voice over the organization of production would represent a weakening of corporate control.

Union leaders have not pressed for more progressive job control demands for two primary reasons. First, such demands are not as likely to yield immediate victories which can enhance the images of these leaders. Second, any battle over such issues is not easily won, for confrontation over shopfloor control threatens to undermine private corporate control over the production process itself--not a prerogative readily given up by management. Consequently, union leaders seeking to maintain political support among their membership search for easier and more immediate ways to make gains.

Union officials tend to emphasize bread-and-butter issues rather than workplace-control issues. Sociologist Richard Hyman refers to the union's trade-off of shopfloor demands for economic gains as a "domestication of union goals" (1975:89). He explains that this tendency may be attributed to the unions' "institutional interest" and the union leaders' personal political interest "in establishing stable bargaining relationships with those controlling significant reserves of social power, and in avoiding aims and actions which might arouse strong hostility and hence jeopardize organizational security" (ibid.:89-90). (This is not to say that economic demands are easily won in union:management negotiations, it is to say that there is less management resistance to such issues because corporate control over production is not threatened.) Thus, according to the neo-Marxists, given unions' place in the social system, they do not really change the social relationships between worker and management; rather, they help to maintain them.

This helps to explain why rank-and-file movements emerge so early in a union. The union does not accomplish many of the workplace reforms that members expect it to accomplish. Disenchantment grows and a movement for social change once again emerges. Nevertheless, given the neo-Marxist view, one might expect these reform movements to either (1) have the same fate as the unions they seek to reform, i.e. be coopted or integrated into the social system without fundamentally altering relationships between labor and capital, or (2) be stopped by coercive means, i.e. expelled from unions or made illegal by civil law.

However, here is where the perspective of this book differs from some neo-Marxist theory. I am arguing that reform is not doomed to failure. By selecting the appropriate organizational forms and political strategies, grassroots leaders can resist cooptive forces. As noted earlier in the discussion of "resource mobilization," social movement leaders and members consciously mold movement organizational structure, strategy, and ideology. Thus, they have some latitude over the success or failure of the social movement organization. By adding this approach to the existing neo-Marxist models, one is able to shield the neo-Marxist perspective from criticisms that it ignores the potential role of movements in bringing about change; it helps to counter the argument that this perspective is crude economic determinism. Before summarizing the overall perspective used in the book, it is helpful to take into consideration two bodies of literature that have frequently been used to explain the existence of leadership oligarchy and the lack of successful reform movements in most American unions.

CAPITALIST INSTITUTIONAL DOMINANCE AND ORGANIZATIONAL THEORY

Some organizational theorists have asserted that there are "natural" tendencies in organizations that predispose them to oligarchy or centralization of power. These theories imply that reform movements are bound to fail as a result of the internal dynamics of organizations alone. Specifically, in *Political Parties* (first published in 1915) Robert Michels pessimistically describes the evolution of intra-organizational reform movements and the resulting organizational changes, as resembling "successive waves" of democratic practice which swell during the initial stages of reform and inevitably deteriorate into aristocracies or oligarchies once the new leaders become entrenched. According to Michels's "iron law of oligarchy," the seeds of self-destruction are to be found within democratic organizations themselves. For Michels, "the principal cause of oligarchy in the democratic parties is to be found in the technical indispensability of leadership" (1962:364). Studying oligarchic tendencies in political organizations, the early twentieth-century theorist elaborates:

> The process which has begun in consequence of the differentiation of functions in the party is completed by a complex of qualities which the leaders acquire through their detachment from the mass. At the outset, leaders rise SPONTANEOUSLY: their functions are ACCESSORY and GRATUITOUS. Soon, however, they become PROFESSIONAL leaders, and in this second stage of development they are STABLE AND IRREMOVABLE [ibid.].

Michels summarizes his argument regarding the inevitability of oligarchy, stating that "it is organization which gives birth to the dominion of the elected over the electors, of the mandararies over the mandators, of the delegates over the delegators. Who says organization says oligarchy" (ibid.:365).

Michels's argument is related, but not identical, to Max Weber's thesis pertaining to professionalization of leaders and bureaucratization of organizations. According to Weber, these developments cause a separation of leaders from their constituencies. Weber states that

> Bureaucracy inevitably accompanies modern *mass* democracy in contrast to the democratic self-government of small homogeneous units. This results from the characteristic principle of bureaucracy: the abstract regularity of the execution of authority, which is a result of the demand of "equality before the law" in the personal and functional sense, hence, of the horror of "privilege," and the principled rejection of doing business from "case to case" [1958a:224].

The leaders of these new organizations become increasingly "professionalized" by virtue of their specialized functions. There then follows a separation between the public on the one hand and the professional politician and bureaucrat on the other hand. According to Weber, this separation is facilitated by the fact "that a relatively small number of men are primarily interested in political life and hence interested in sharing political power" (1958b:99).

However, both Michels's and Weber's perspectives view organizations in isolation from the broader political economy (see Benson [1977] and Wright [1974]). This narrow focus can be misleading.* What may seem to be "natural laws" of organization may in fact be the products of the nature of the political economy at a particular time in history. Relevant to this point are a number of neo-Marxist criticisms of classical organizational theory. First, classic theory has been criticized for ignoring social class, social stratification, and social conflict (Goldman & VanHouten 1977:111). Second, because work groups and individual organizations have been the basic units of analysis in much of the organizational literature, there has been "little discussion of how the economy, the political context, or the community affects day-to-day organizational life" (ibid.:111-12). Finally, organizational literature has been somewhat ahistorical and has not clearly described changes within organizations or alterations in the organization-environment relationship (e.g., Heydebrand 1977).

---

* While Michels and Max Weber do appear to have similar views, it should be noted that there is a fundamental difference in their perspectives. Michels looked more at the process of democracy, or its antithesis, oligarchy. Weber looked more at professionalization of leadership and bureaucratization. He saw that these developments could undermine democracy, but that they did not necessarily do so. This is further discussed in Scaff (1981:1282).

One consequence of this has been the tendency of organizational theory to be "undialectical, seldom seeing the roots of tomorrow in the reality of today" (Goldman & VanHouten 1977:111-12). These criticisms of traditional organizational literature and the modified perspective that they imply will be used to guide the analysis used throughout this book.

Capitalist Institutional Dominance and Pluralism

It is difficult to construct any theory related to union reform without reference to the classic pluralist sociological study of unions, *Union Democracy*, by Seymour Martin Lipset, Martin Trow, and James Coleman (1956). The authors of the study of the International Typographical Union argue that organizational responsiveness to grassroots sentiment, or "democracy," depends on the strength of intermediate social structures which link the individual union member to his organization.[2] They suggest that

> democracy is most likely to become institutionalized in organizations whose members form organized or structured subgroups which while maintaining a basic loyalty to the larger organization, constitute relatively independent and autonomous centers of power in the organization. Or to put it another way, democracy is strengthened when members are not only related to the larger organization but are also affiliated with or loyal to subgroups within the organization [p. 15].

Therefore, in the context of the present study, they are arguing that the likelihood that rank-and-file insurgencies will have an impact on union structure and policy and be successful depends on the presence of mediating structures. Mediating social structures may include intra- or extra-union political groups and social organizations, as well as social networks that are nurtured by workplace job structures, work hours, and residential patterns. Lipset et al. argue that the oligarchic characteristic of many American trade unions is a function of the absence of "occupational community" and the absence of the related intermediate groups that foster "democracy." They assert that unlike the social homogeneity of printers and their "occupational community," most occupational settings do not have the social homogeneity needed to support democratic processes.

I make reference to the pluralist perspective here not so much to criticize it, but to argue that it can be integrated into the capitalist institutional dominance model. Clearly, there is a need for structures which mediate between rank-and-filer and union official if leadership responsiveness is to be developed and maintained. Moreover, in the case of the reform movement itself, similar links between leader and supporter need to be maintained if the movement is to spread and resist cooptation. The only difference between my perspective and that of Lipset et al. is that I would make more explicit the potential for *creating* occupational community and other intermediate links between leader and grassroots worker, whereas they imply that only intermediate links that occur *naturally* will contribute to union democracy.

CAPITALIST INSTITUTIONAL DOMINANCE MODEL: A SUMMARY

The present research is guided by a model combining a number of complementary theoretical views. As outlined in the preceding pages, elements of the neo-Marxist view of political economy and the pluralist model of organizational democracy can be combined to help one to better understand rank-and-file reform movements in trade unions. The political economy perspective provides an understanding of the broad social, economic, and political factors, *outside* of an organization which can inhibit, or at least influence, the development of rank-and-file reform movements. The pluralist model looks at structures *inside* organizations.

By supplementing these perspectives with the resource mobilization theory, these extra- and intra-organizational factors do not appear as immutable as the neo-Marxist and pluralist perspectives sometimes imply. Resource mobilization theory argues that organizational structures and strategies--consciously adopted by social movement organizations--can affect the success of a movement. While a rank-and-file reform organization might be bucking strong pressures from dominant social institutions, this perspective indicates that failure is not a forgone conclusion. Specifically, if a movement can mobilize resources and nurture social solidarity or "occupational community," it can counteract organizational tendencies toward oligarchy, bureaucratization, and leadership professionalization. In essence, a successful movement is one which seeks to strengthen the social links between grassroots union members and union leaders as a way of resisting cooptive pressures in our political economy.

Specifically, one can identify three social groups relevant to understanding union organizational processes and structure. The three groups are management, union leadership, and rank-and-file workers. Union leadership mediates between the other two groups (see Figure 1.1). One can characterize the social process as a "tug-of-war" with union members pulling union leaders from one direction and management pulling union leaders from the other direction. The strength of the "rope" between union members and union leaders is determined by the quality of intermediate social links. The strength of the "rope" between managment and union leaders is determined by the level of domination by monopoly capital institutions. Neo-Marxists are particularly concerned with the relationship between mangement and union leaders. To them dominant forces in the capitalist political economy exert pressure on union leaders, bringing them closer to the interests of monopoly capital. On the other hand, pluralists concentrate on the relationship between union leadership and rank-and-file workers. They focus on the role of intra-organizational intermediate groups in linking union leaders' policies to rank-and-file interests.

If one adds progressive rank-and-file movement organizations to this figure, they ostensibly work to strengthen the link between union member and union leader. However, the extent to which the movement and movement organizations strengthen this link is a function of the movement's own characteristics. These characteristics, in turn, are influenced by the same political economic forces that influence the union itself. Rank-and-file movements are not immune to the influences of other social institutions. In their everyday roles in the workplace and in society, as well as in their overall socialization, workers are subject to the influences of the overall political economy. Thus the reform organizations they create affect, and are affected by, the existing social, economic, and political arrangements. It is with this perspective that we begin the case study.

ORGANIZATION OF THE CHAPTERS

The chapters are divided into five chronological periods which correspond to changes in both the characteristics within and the social relationships between the steel industry, the Steelworkers union, and the rank-and-file movement. Primary characteristics of the industry which are studied include the presence of industrial growth or contraction (e.g. employment and investment), profit rates, automation, and industrial structure (e.g. concentration of ownership and diversification of holdings). Primary characteristics related to internal union structure and to nature of industrial relations are the homogeneity *versus* the heterogeneity of union membership characteristics, international *versus* local control over union decision-making, centralization *versus* decentralization of collective bargaining structure, cooperation *versus* conflict in industrial relations, real wage and benefit levels, and changes in union members' workplace rights. Primary characteristics related to the examination of the rank-and-file movement include level of organization (local *versus* unionwide), strategies (e.g. organizing local unionists *versus* coordinating unionwide activity), and issues (e.g. "union democracy" and improvement in working conditions).

The five chronological periods are as follows:

1. Period One: Initial Union Organization (1936-1947)

2. Period Two: Wage Growth and Local Autonomy (1947-1959)

3. Period Three: Wage Stabilization and Union Centralization (1959-1973)

4. Period Four: Official Industrial Peace, Improved Wages, Further Union Membership Diversification and the Rise in Rank-and-File Activity (1973-1979)

5. Period Five: Industrial Contraction in Steel and Decline in Rank-and-File Activity (1979-present)

Chapter 2 covers Period One during which the union was organized and the rank-and-file movement was just emerging. In the early years of Period One the rank-and-file movement was indistinguishable from the nascent union itself. Chapter 3 covers Period Two when the local autonomy movement emerged, but had only a limited impact on unionwide policy making. Chapter 4 looks at a third period which saw significant changes in union structure, industrial structure, labor relations, and wage trends. The union was becoming more centralized,the industry more automated, and real wage levels stabilized. The rank-and-file movement, still based in autonomous pockets scattered throughout the union in the early years of this period, started to grow toward the end of this period. Period Four, which is analyzed in Chapters 5 and 6, saw the strongest rank-and-file movement in the union's history. These chapters contain a detailed analysis of the strengths and weaknesses of recently formed social movement organizations--most notably the organization and networks behind Edward Sadlowski's campaigns for Director of the Chicago USWA District and later for USWA International President. Chapter 7 looks at the subsequent decline of the rank-and-file movement, apparent diversification of union membership, and contraction of the steel industry. Finally, Chapter 8 discusses the implications of the case study for social movement and organizational theory. This last chapter also examines the potential for future growth of the rank-and-file reform movement, given changes in the industrial, economic, and social structure of the 1980s.

Chapter 2

Union Organization and Industry Growth
1936–1947

The 1930s represented watershed years for labor relations in the steel industry. The United Steelworkers of America was born in the social turmoil of the Great Depression along with a number of other industrial unions. The emergence of the union was the result of a variety of factors related to changing social, political, and economic processes related to the growth of monopoly capitalism. The early years of the union were characterized by an adversarial relationship with management and a relatively high level of rank-and-file participation in union organizing and policy making. However, by the late 1940s, union leaders were developing a more "civil" relationship with industry. The union itself was being shaped by dominant capitalist institutions; by the late 1940s there were a number of indicators that the union leadership was being integrated into monopoly capital industrial relations. It was at this time that a rank-and-file movement first emerged in the USWA. The early movement was concentrated at the local level and was a reaction to what many members saw as the drift of union leaders away from rank-and-file interests and the threat of centralized administration to local union control.

THE INDUSTRY

By the 1930s, the steel industry had gone through a number of transformations since its development in the 19th century. The fragmented production and decentralized ownership that characterized the industry of the 19th century became more integrated and centralized with the increased demand for steel in the late 19th and early 20th centuries (D. Brody 1969; Hogan 1971; Stone 1975). This consolidation of the steel industry was characteristic of economic and social trends in basic industries during the historical transition from an era of competitive capital to a period of monopoly capital (Edwards 1979; Stone 1975). Throughout the late 19th and early 20th centuries, a large number of small steel companies were integrated into larger corporations such as U.S. Steel, American Bridge, Bethlehem Steel, Republic Steel, Jones and Laughlin, National Steel, Youngstown Sheet and Tube, and Armco Steel. By the 1920s, new steel corporations were well established and were expanding their production capacity. Despite some fluctuation in demand during this decade, the 1920s were years of economic growth for the steel industry (Hogan 1971:3:878).

However, during the Great Depression, the steel industry was hit as hard as other basic industries. Production and new investments fell precipitously during this period and did not recover until 1940 when demand increased with the start of World War II in Europe. William T. Hogan, a prominent economic historian of the American steel industry, observes that the 1930s and 1940s were decades of contrast which "saw both the depths of steel operation in 1932 and its height in 1944" (ibid.:1193). It was in the environment of the 1930s economic upheaval--with its wage cuts and massive layoffs for workers--that the first successful industrial union in basic steel emerged. Changes in the structure of the workplace and changes in the characteristics of the workforce that accompanied the growth of monopoly capital produced a social environment in which such economic upheaval stimulated a grassroots union movement.

CHANGES IN THE CHARACTER OF LABOR UNDER MONOPOLY CAPITAL

Prior to the development of monopoly capital control in the American steel industry, the workplace was characterized by a high degree of worker autonomy in the workplace. In the 1800s, craftsmen and the helpers they hired occupied key positions in the production process. Their knowledge of the work process, their control over work on the shopfloor, and the relatively strong influence of their craft unions, provided them with considerable power and leverage when dealing with employers. However, with the development of monopoly capital came deskilling of the steel workforce along with diminished craft union power.

This rationalization of the work process and weakening of the skilled workers' union--which was apparent with the industry's defeat of the Amalgamated Association of Iron Steel and Tin Workers (AAISTW) in the 1892 Homestead, Pennsylvania strike--established a new relationship between labor and capital. Harry Braverman (1974), in *Labor and Monopoly Capital*, and Richard Edwards (1979), in *Contested Terrain*, have described this new era as one where employers seek to more systematically regulate the production process--particularly by instituting better control over the workforce. A key aspect of this rationalization is the employer's effort to gain more control over both (1) the knowledge of how the production process is completed and (2) decision-making on the shopfloor. Introduction of new machinery along with an increase in the proportion of semi-skilled and unskilled workers not only increases productivity within the industry, but it reduces the workplace control exerted by craftsmen. In the steel industry, these changes, such as the introduction of foremen, took place in the first decades of the 20th century (Stone 1975).

However, at the same time as steel companies were increasing their control through rationalization of the work process, they were creating a larger, more homogeneous workforce, i.e. more homogeneous in terms of skill levels. It was this unification of the workforce which ultimately set the stage for the development of an industrial union and the elimination of the craft union mentality which had been a divisive factor among steelworkers for decades.* In addition, forces which had inhibited the growth of unions in earlier

---

* Analysis of the Great Steel Strike of 1919 shows that during the transition from competitive capital work relations of the 19th century to work relations characteristic of full-fledged monopoly capital structures of the 1930s, vestiges of craft unionism combined with more "repressive" social forces, e.g. government anti-unionism and anti-radicalism, to frustrate grassroots union movements in the steel industry (Foster 1971; Interchurch World Movement 1920).

decades, e.g. anti-radicalism and government opposition to unions, were overshadowed by the upheaval of the Great Depression and the progressive politics associated with Franklin D. Roosevelt's New Deal.[1]

A GRASSROOTS UNION MOVEMENT

The surge in the industrial union movement of the 1930s was a product of the social, political and economic environment of the Great Depression. In the early years of the Depression, there were massive layoffs and major cuts in wages for those steelworkers still working. Steel employment between 1929 and 1933 declined from 454,000 to 254,000.[2] The common wage rate dropped from an average of 44 cents per hour in the late 1920s to 33 cents per hour in 1931-32 (Hogan 1971:3:1167). However, by 1934, employment and wages started to increase once again. In contrast to the low employment mark of 254,000 in 1933, the number of steelworkers reached 544,000 by 1937 (ibid.:1181). It was at this point that workers were particularly receptive to unionization.

Continued disenchantment with job displacement, wage reduction, and the concomitant decline in living standards of the early 1930s combined with the apparent turnaround in the economy to produce an economic and social stability which emboldened workers to be more militant. Many workers, who had been just trying to "cope" during the Depression, now felt more secure and sought to bring about significant improvements in their living and working conditions. Sociologists have noted that social conflict often arises when a recessionary period is followed by an upturn. According to theorists such as Anthony Oberschall (1973) and Mancur Olson (1963), this conflict emerges because some social groups do not believe they are receiving their fair share of social and financial rewards produced by the upturn. Oberschall points out that "in early phases of economic growth, there is a tendency for increased inequality of incomes to come about" (p. 38). He adds that this is usually a product of the "reluctance of employers to restore wage levels" to pre-depression levels and instead reap higher profits to compensate for losses (ibid.:41-42).

In the present case, the steel companies were reaping the benefits of the economic upturn, while steelworkers did not perceive that they were experiencing a proportionate improvement in working conditions and wages. For example, U.S. Steel earned profits of $50.5 million and $94.9 million in 1936 and 1937 respectively; these figures represented significant improvements compared to the losses or minute profits of the 1932-35 period. The index of overall output per man hour (1929=100) was up from 91.8 in 1931 to 112.0 in 1936 (Hogan 1971:3:1205). However, at the same time, workers' demands for a substantial increase in wages were not met by the companies (ibid.:1172). Therefore, it appears that two factors contributed to increased grassroots support for unionization during the mid-1930s. First, there was a feeling among workers that employment opportunites were once again stable or increasing, thus freeing workers from the threat of job loss. Second, anti-company sentiment grew as workers perceived that wages and working conditions were not improving as rapidly as was the overall recovery of the industry.

The Steel Workers Organizing Committee

It was in this atmosphere that the Committee of Industrial Organization (CIO) emerged under the leadership of John L. Lewis. The Steel Workers Organizing Committee (SWOC)--the precursor of the United Steelworkers of America (USWA)--was part of the new CIO and was formed in 1936. However, it would be incorrect to interpret the development of industrial unionism in the steel industry as merely a "top-down" process where CIO-appointed leaders and organizers had to convince workers to join the new union. While there is no doubt that CIO leadership was instrumental in the growth of SWOC after its formation in 1936, it was facilitated by the spontaneous grassroots union organizing that was already taking place. In 1934, a rank-and-file movement to convert what was left of the AAISTW into an aggressive industrial union had emerged. Another small but growing union--the Steel and Metal Workers Industrial Union (SMWIU)--had also been organized in the early 1930s.*

Perhaps the most significant indicator of grassroots involvement in the 1930s industrial movement, was worker resistance to "company unions." In the mid-1930s, steel companies attempted to sidetrack the emerging union movement by forming friendly "company unions" or "employee representation plans." However, in many cases rank-and-file activists undermined these unions. Independent from any central coordinating organization, workers in a number of steel plants took over company unions or had them disbanded. Historian Irving Bernstein explains that between 1934 and 1936 company unions--which covered over 90 percent of the employees in the steel industry (Harbison 1938:1)--

> grew progressively more independent of management and made ever-growing demands both for worker control over the organizations and for higher wages and improved conditions.... Aggressive company union leaders emerged and they made significant substantive gains [1971:455-56].

---

* Linda Nyden, "The History of the Steel and Metal Workers Industrial Union," mimeographed paper, 1973.

These company unions provided the foundation for SWOC. For example, in the Chicago area, worker-controlled company unions at the Inland Steel plant in East Chicago and the Illinois Steel facilities in Chicago and Gary banded together to form the Calumet Council, which was later integrated into the Steelworkers union.

Once SWOC was formed, it relied heavily on already-existing local activist networks in its organizing drive. A prominent example of SWOC's integration of existing shopfloor worker networks into the union was their use of Communist Party organizers to do local recruiting. Before 1936, the Party had been active in establishing local councils of employed workers. Once the economy picked up and workers returned to their jobs, many of these councils and the social networks they represented were brought into the union. George Kimbley, a SWOC organizer in Gary, Indiana, recalls that the union worked with activists who had built neighborhood Communist Councils. He explains that local Party members "had a nucleus set up" before SWOC came to the area. Joe Norrick, another SWOC organizer who helped organize Indiana Harbor's Inland Steel and Youngstown Sheet and Tube works, remarks that the CP was instrumental in organizing these key plants in the Chicago area.

SWOC also capitalized on support from local ethnic societies and Black community organizations. Italian, Polish, Serbian, Croatian, Mexican, Hungarian, and other ethnic lodges provided a base for union organization. The National Negro Congress, through its local committees, was instrumental in bringing Blacks into the union (Kimbley). Since most members of these fraternal groups worked in the mills, such organizations helped to bring in a large number of members at the same time.

Steelworkers involved in organizing the union recall little resistance to the union; grassroots support appeared to be spontaneous. George Patterson, a Chicago steelworker who became a full-time SWOC organizer after his success in establishing the Calumet Council, commented that most of the new members of SWOC were "joining up on their own volition" and did not need much convincing by the union organizers (Lynd & Lynd 1973:94). John Sargent, the first president of USWA Local 1010 at Inland Steel's East Chicago plant, recalls that since steelworkers

> were ready to accept a change, it was not a difficult task to organize the people in the steel mills. Thousands upon thousands of them, in a spontaneous movement, joined the steelworkers' organization at that time. And they did it because conditions in the mill were terrible and because they had become disgusted with the political set-up in this country [ibid.:106].

Emergence of a Leadership:Rank-and-File Rift

In the early organizing days of the Steelworkers union, the grassroots worker movement and union were synonymous. In the period preceding the establishment of union:company contracts, membership recruitment was vital to the growth of unions. The local networks of grassroots workers as well as the individuals capable of recruiting them into the union were all-important. The early union movement was characterized by a "missionary spirit." One could not distinguish between a "rank-and-file reform movement" and a more conservative union leadership. However, as the union organization grew and contracts with companies were established, a formal labor relations system was created.

At this point the interests of union leader and rank-and-file member begin to diverge. Richard A. Lester, author of *As Unions Mature*, explains this process. He notes that, at first, unions

> must fight for existence as well as [for] goals that generally are considered radical. Under the circumstances membership participation is likely to be high and leadership positions in the organization are apt to be won by the agitator and the table pounder [1958:21].

However, when unions gain acceptance from industry, a transformation occurs in the organization's goals, leadership, internal structure, and internal distribution of power. As Lester explains,

> Instead of pursuing a crusade against the "enemy," it cooperates increasingly with other groups in industry, government, and society.... The need for specialists becomes more pressing, a hierarchy and bureaucracy tend to develop, and the relationship of top officials to the rank-and-file grows more impersonal. Some functions and decisions shift from the local to higher levels in the organization [ibid.:21-22].

It is at this point that a conflict between top union leaders and grassroots activists emerges. Cooperation between union and company and the institutionalization of a centrally administered labor relations system represent a shift away from the informal rank-and-file worker-influenced system existing on the shopfloor during the organizing days and early years of the union.

Ad Hoc Shopfloor Labor Relations

During the 1930s, before company:union contracts were established, the rank and file's use of strikes, lasting a few hours and involving a few workers in a particular work setting, was an effective method of pressuring company officials to expedite settlement of workplace grievances. This ad hoc bargaining system often yielded decisions favorable to workers. Joe Gyurko, a steelworker at Inland Steel's Indiana Harbor Works since the 1930s, recalls that in the 1936-42 pre-contract period, departmental strikes were common. When foremen or supervisors refused to deal with pressing issues affecting working conditions, the men thought nothing of stopping work and letting gondolas full of molten steel hang in mid-air. In these situations the rapidly approaching danger that production would be interrupted in order to clean out the gondola and reheat the steel acted as a time clock forcing the company to bargain with the workers. More often than not, the supervisors settled with departmental workers before much production time was lost (Gyurko).

This instant grievance settlement procedure won significant gains for steelworkers during the early years of SWOC prior to the signing of contracts. Studying this period, historian Edward Zivich found that

> Free from the "no-strike" clause and institutionalized, upper-level, industry-wide collective bargaining characteristic of later years, the local union enjoyed a six-year period of success unequaled in its subsequent history. Through a variety of militant "on-the-job" actions and strikes, particularly as military orders increased the need for uninterrupted production, the union secured unprecedented improvements in wages and working conditions for the Harbor work force.*

Zivich adds that these strikes were not merely actions initiated by the local leadership, but rather "were primarily movements from below (p. 37).[3]

It was this grassroots involvement that was discouraged once the union became well established in the industry. However, it was not an internal organizational process that caused the reduced responsiveness of leaders to rank-and-filers--as Lester would have us believe. Rather, the institutionalization of centralized labor relations and the resultant decline in membership voice was a function of social processes in the broader political economy.

----

* Edward A. Zivich, "Fighting Union: The CIO at Inland Steel, 1936-1942" (Master's thesis, University of Wisconsin-Milwaukee, 1972), pp. 2-3.

POLITICAL ECONOMY OF RATIONALIZATION AND SOCIAL CONTROL

As the union became more established, ad hoc bargaining was replaced by more formal arrangements. The union side of labor relations moved away from the immediate workplace and up the union hierarchy. The union hierarchy increasingly took on a social control function; it worked to harness grassroots militancy rather than stimulate it. The union also began to serve a positive function for industry in the sense that labor relations became more predictable. Contracts prohibited strikes during the life of the agreement, and hence allowed companies to more accurately estimate future costs and production levels. Union:management agreements rationalized the job classification system, pay scales, work hours, promotion patterns and grievance procedures which reduced many sources of day-to-day disagreements and increased productivity. In "The Origins of Job Structures in the Steel Industry," Katherine Stone (1975:150-51) argues that the union helped the industry to rationalize an "exceedingly complex and chaotic" wage structure.[4] This rationalization process derailed the grassroots-based informal grievance system. Union officials, not the rank and file, came to control the system. Consequently, the rank and file and the leadership were increasingly at odds over who should control decision making. Therefore, the rationalization process and the resulting emergence of a rank-and-file movement distinct from the union leadership was the product of broad political economic forces and not merely the result of internal organizational processes.

Even though trade unions represent the organizational outgrowth of grassroots worker movements challenging management prerogatives in the workplace, unions are themselves influenced by the political economy. A number of writers have pointed out that unions often come to serve the interests of the employers (Aronowitz, 1973; Averitt 1968; Hyman 1975; Stone 1975). Although corporate resistance to major industrial union organizing efforts of the Depression was substantial, the institutional arrangements that emerged ultimately benefited industry. In return for higher wages, fringe benefits, and better working conditions, the union provides management with guarantees of a stable, predictable, and productive workforce. Largely unfettered by labor conflict, monopoly capital is, therefore, able to expand more freely.

Dual economy theorist Robert T. Averitt (1968: 145-47, 152) suggests that the union guarantees functional for industry are as follows:

1. *Uniformity of wage rates and reduction of labor turnover.* The emergence of pattern bargaining removes wage competition between companies in an industry and reduces labor turnover.

2. *Predictable labor costs.* Collective bargaining insures employers against unforeseen wage increases. It allows them to plan labor costs for the life of the contract.

3. *Protection from wildcat work stoppages.* Unions agree not to strike during the life of the contract, choosing instead to handle individual complaints within a grievance procedure. The union, as well as the company, becomes a social control agent which levies sanctions against workers violating these rules, e.g. the union will not necessarily oppose the firing of a worker who violates the contract by organizing a wildcat strike.

4. *Increased productivity.* Reduction in wildcat stoppages, the inclusion of productivity provisions in union:management contracts, and the adoption of contract provisions guaranteeing union cooperation in plant automation, all contribute to increased productivity.

Unions, particularly union leaders, have been incorporated into the system of shopfloor social control. The grievance procedure and no-strike provisions in union contracts are legal systems guaranteeing union cooperation.

These functions and characteristics of unions did not develop overnight. The role of unions as partners in the rationalization and social control of the industrial work force developed over a number of decades and took different forms at different times. This process will be examined in the next few chapters. What is important to understand at this point, is that during the 1936-47 period these functions of the USWA first became apparent. At this time, the industry started to put pressure on the union to have labor relations decisions made by union representatives as far removed from the actual workplace as possible. This was done in an effort to (1) moderate the influence of parochial interests that might be divisive in longterm planning in the industry and (2) prevent the injection of shopfloor workers' more militant proposals into the collective bargaining process. There was also pressure to bargain at national, industry-wide levels so that labor relations could be standardized. In an industry where companies have national markets, such standardization facilitates planning and regulation of the labor force. In an article which examines the history of collective bargaining in steel, Richard Betheil observes that during the 1942-46 period, management was actively seeking to control the steel workforce by enlisting the help of USWA International officials (1978:3). It was this social process which caused leaders--particularly those at top levels--to drift away from the grassroots workers movement out of which the union had emerged. Thus, the stage was set for conflict between the new union's leadership and its rank and file.

THE EARLY RANK-AND-FILE MOVEMENT

The early grassroots movement challenging the International leadership was a group of autonomous local networks rather than a well-organized national organization. Decentralization of union policy-making and collective bargaining were the major issues of the early movement. This structure and emphasis was not surprising since much of the bargaining and many of the administrative decisions during the early years were still made at the local level. The movement was an effort to stop the erosion of local control. Local activists also had an incentive to protect the autonomy of the local union because that was their political power base.

Although adherence to this same structure by rank-and-file groups in the 1960s and 1970s was a primary source of weakness (as will be described in later chapters), the decentralized nature of the movement in the 1940s was not entirely a liability. Since contracts were generally locally negotiated (or at least negotiated company by company), local unions did have more influence over labor relations and contract enforcement than they do today. For example, at Inland Steel in East Chicago, Indiana, negotiations were close to the membership. According to Joe Gyurko, a union leader at the time, the union and company negotiated

> right at the main office building in the Harbor [Indiana Harbor, a section of East Chicago]. We used to have a picket line around Plant One and around the main office building. John Sargent [the Local 1010 President] would open up the window and tell us how the negotiations were coming along [Gyurko].

Even after contracts were signed, local unions continued to be involved in the industrial relations process. They would often pressure the company through the use of job actions, e.g. wildcat strikes and slowdowns, despite the fact that such actions violated the contract. At times the International union had little control over labor relations at the local level: for example, USWA District 31 files show a number of instances where companies and top International or District officials exchanged telegrams trying to determine how to control local union members and leaders. Thus, the emergent local rank-and-file movement did have an impact on union politics and industrial relations at this time. To understand the overall rank-and-file movement one needs to understand the character of local rank-and-file caucuses at that time. Moreover to understand the evolution of the rank-and-file movement into its present form, one needs to understand changes in local rank-and-file caucuses--the building blocks of the rank-and-file movement--and how they are related to the broader union.

CASE STUDY OF A LOCAL UNION CAUCUS

To analyze the nature of local rank-and-file groups, the political activity in one local union has been selected. Rather than select a local union that is "representative" of all union locals, I have chosen one local that provides the strongest history of rank-and-file activity. Local 1010, which represents workers at Inland Steel's East Chicago, Indiana plant, will be used because the Local 1010 Rank and File Caucus was one of the earliest components of the grassroots-based autonomist movement of the early 1940s. Forty years later, it continues to function as an organizational force in the Steelworkers rank-and-file movement. Also, since it was formed, the Rank and File Caucus has succeeded--at various times--in getting its candidates elected to local union office and its programs transformed into local union policy.

Grassroots participation in Local 1010 politics has been greater than rank-and-file involvement in other USWA locals. In part, this is due to the fact that the local was organized by individuals already working in the plant, rather than by "outsiders"--organizers from other locals, who were assigned by the International union leadership. Most of these indigenous organizers became key figures in local union politics once the local union was organized and recognized by the company. Many were elected to union office. Moreover, given the early commitment to grassroots involvement, many of these early leaders helped to formulate local union by-laws which protected and encouraged continued rank-and-file involvement in local union decision making. These made union offices, such as departmental assistant grievers, safety stewards, and committee heads, elected offices. In contrast, most USWA locals fill these offices by appointment. While militant unionists were not able to maintain constant control over local union offices--particularly during the McCarthy era of the early 1950s--the democratic mechanisms established in the first years of the local union served to stimulate a high level of grassroots involvement in local politics. Also, the institutionalization of local rank-and-file social networks into the Local 1010 Rank-and-File Caucus facilitated grassroots participation at the East Chicago local union.* Nevertheless,

---

* Although the word "caucus" has connotations of an ad hoc group within a political organization or legislative body, the word has broader meaning in my analysis of rank-and-file politics in the USWA. It is used to describe this more informal and ad hoc grouping; however, it is also used to describe more formal, longer-lasting insurgent organizations. This second meaning to the word was more widely used in the 1960s and 1970s. At this time "caucus" more often than not referred to a group that had some structure beyond a social network. Such caucuses often had formal structures, members consciously made decisions with the future of the caucus in

like the broader rank-and-file movement, the Local 1010 Caucus and other local union rank-and-file caucuses like it have gone through metamorphoses during each of the historical periods outlined in this book.

Social Networks

The early Local 1010 Rank and File Caucus is best described as a loosely structured organization which was led by three or four prominent activists. It did not have the elected leadership, large membership, regular meetings, and regular publications that the Caucus of the 1970s adopted. According to Mary Hopper, who has been involved in union politics since the 1940s, the early Caucus "wasn't as widespread as it is now. They were a small select handfull of people.... They kept their tight little group (Hopper). When it needed to mobilize broad support, the "tight little group" fanned out through the mill to rally support from fellow workers.

In many ways, the more formal organizational structure developed by the Caucus in the 1970s, was not needed during this period. The young union organization of the 1940s was characterized by much greater grassroots participation than the union of the 1970s. It did not take much effort to get workers to attend a meeting in the early days. The organizing zeal and "missionary spirit" were still very much present. This spirit, took the place of formalized structures in mobilizing support. Also, because many of the Caucus leaders had helped to organize the local union, they occupied key positions in workplace social networks and could easily stimulate grassroots activity.

Limited Interest in Unionwide Issues

At the same time the informal and decentralized nature of the early rank-and-file movement made it difficult for any unionwide movement to emerge--that is, a movement which might have prevented increasing centralization of organizational decision-making. Decisions to centralize the union were being made at International union levels where the rank-and-file movement had little influence. The transformation of informal networks into a unionwide organization would have required a major change in consciousness. Organizers and local union leaders were skilled at organizing in workplaces of a few hundred employees and meeting with small groups of workers in taverns and homes. They were used to discussing pressing local workplace issues, not unionwide issues. They did not possess the skills needed to help the movement flourish at levels higher than the local union.

---

mind, and opponents and incumbent union officials treated them as mini-political parties.

Furthermore, what would be the reason for local activists to turn their attention to unionwide organizing? Even though their ability to control union policies was slowly being eroded by centralization of decision making, they continued to receive support from their local followers. There still were local issues over which to battle. As long as there were a significant number of decisions made at the local level, it did not make sense to take attention away from local politicking and invest time in the difficult task of broadening the movement.

Another factor anchoring the 1010 Rank and File Caucus to local rather than unionwide politics was the structure of the industry itself. Inland Steel had only one basic steel producing facility, unlike companies such as U.S. Steel that had numerous plants around the country. Therefore, Local 1010 had more leverage over their company than did U.S. Steel locals over their employer. Locals representing one plant of a multi-plant company either would have to band together or work through the International if they wanted to have an impact on union:company policy. While this factor alone does not explain why progressive rank-and-file caucuses emerge, it does explain why the 1010 Caucus remained in the forefront of the movement. It may also explain why the 1010 Rank and File Caucus did not quickly move to form a unionwide network directed at changing International policy.

A FRAGMENTED RANK-AND-FILE MOVEMENT

The movement's concentration on local union activity and the absence of any coherent national organization left militant unionists relatively powerless at national conventions. This gave the International leadership the opportunity to eat away at local autonomy. For example, at the 1937 Wage and Policy Convention--where the newly organized unionists had their first opportunity to make recommendations on national union policy--none of the local autonomists' resolutions received approval from the convention (Ulman 1962:30). Instead of passing resolutions favoring decentralization of organizational decision-making, the early meeting established a set of rules allowing for greater centralization.

It was after this first official meeting of SWOC that the battle lines between leaders and a more militant group of rank-and-filers began to emerge. By the 1940s, dissident groups of steelworkers in the major industrial areas had formed "steel councils." These alliances brought representatives from both small and large rank-and-file groups into loose coalitions to oppose incumbent District and International leaders (ibid.:36). The Councils represented a visible split between the local union leadership and the International union leadership. However, these limited attempts at coordinating activities of locally based rank-and-file groups did not succeed in stopping the growth in centralized control.   In fact, it was the highly decentralized and fragmented nature of the rank-and-file movement that weakened it in the late 1940s and early 1950s.   As will be shown in the next chapter, this second stage in union development saw a decline in visible rank-and-file activity.

CONCLUSIONS

Grassroots involvement in the early organization of the union served to fuel the rank and file's expectations regarding gains in wages, improvement of workplace rights, and local control over the union.   However, as the union:management relationship became more institutionalized and the rank-and-file voice in union policy and collective bargaining started to diminish, conflict between rank-and-file worker and union leader became apparent.   Because of the continued salience of local union issues, the emergent rank-and-file movement remained decentralized.   Thus, without a well-organized rank-and-file movement at a unionwide level, the top union leadership was able to slowly centralize leadership functions. This internal centralization was as much a response to extra-organizational influences, e.g. pressure from industry, as it was to intra-organizational processes, e.g. pressure from International union leaders seeking to consolidate their control. This character of union leadership development is consistent with the institutional dominance model discussed in the first chapter.   The political and economic environment in which the union was functioning--one one characterized by monopoly capital control--was pulling top leaders away from the rank and file.   As shown in the next chapter, this trend continued through the late 1940s and throughout the 1950s.

Chapter 3

Prosperity and Local Autonomy
1947–1959

The post-war prosperity provided the steel industry with the economic cushion from which to finance wage increases. It was also willing to tolerate some local union autonomy in setting workplace standards as long as it meant steady levels of production. Because of rising real wages and the existence of some local autonomy, grassroots disenchantment was kept to a minimum. What disenchantment did exist remained focused at the local level. The top union leadership was adopting a more cooperative stance with the industry. At the same time, the International officers were further consolidating their control over the union. When a rank-and-file reform organization did emerge in the mid-1950s, it was weak, due to the lack of any strong network of local union groups, limited grassroots disenchantment, and opposition from International officials. Nevertheless, the development of an organization seeking to elect candidates to International office did represent a changing consciousness among dissidents. Unionwide issues were becoming more important among rank-and-file activists.

However, this alone was not enough to strengthen the movement; rank-and-file groups were still using local strategies to fight political battles at the unionwide level.

THE INDUSTRY

The period immediately after World War II was one of prosperity for the steel industry. While the late 1940s represented a shaky period of adjustment from wartime demand to peacetime demand, in the 1950s the industry saw expanded capacity and increased profits. Steel-consuming industries such as auto, construction, and appliance manufacturers, grew after the war. During the late 1940s, there was some debate within the industry over whether or not to increase raw steel capacity. However by the early 1950s--with the combined demand from the expanding domestic consumer market and production for the Korean War--the industry initiated expansion programs. Between 1950 and 1960 the steel industry increased its capacity by almost 50 percent, from 99.4 to 148.6 million tons (Hogan 1971:4:1449-50). Much of the increase was due to construction of new open hearth and electric furnaces. As Table 3.1 shows, steel furnace capacity increased steadily from 1947; a large proportion of the expansion occurred in the Midwest and West away from the older steel-producing centers of Pennsylvania and Ohio (ibid.:1451-54).

Expanding capacity and the resulting increased steel production in the post-war period helped to increase steel industry profits. In 9 out of the 12 years from 1947 to 1958, steel industry profits exceeded 6 percent. (The profit rate is defined here as steel industry after-tax profits as a percent of total revenue.) In contrast, in the 23-year period from 1959 to 1981, the six percent mark was achieved only twice (see Table 3.2). Moreover, in the three-year period 1955-1957, steel profit rates were higher than the manufacturing average--even though steel industry profits traditionally have been lower than most manufacturing industries.[1]

Given relatively high profit rates, expanding market, and limited competition from foreign producers, the industry was not under immediate pressure to stem the sharp rise in wage rates or to further rationalize its control over the workplace. Because of its prosperity, the industry could afford to "buy" industrial peace by providing high wages and limited local workplace autonomy to local unionists. While steel companies did ultimately stabilize wages and increase workplace control after 1959, the industry's primary task in the 1950s was to continue the institutionalization of the union:management relationship established in the previous decade.

STRENGTHENING THE TIE BETWEEN INDUSTRY AND UNION

Between 1947 and 1959, the earlier, more spirited adversarial relationship between company and union evolved into a more stable and cooperative labor relations process.   According to William Hogan, by 1946 "the union had become an accepted institution."   After this period, labor relations were characterized by "a general atmosphere of cooperation" (1971:4:1614, 1616).   Collective bargaining became more centralized and contract agreements were standardized.   Top union officials increasingly took over the role of collective bargaining agents for local unions.   "Pattern bargaining" was adopted by union and industry.   This meant that the contract settlement between the USWA and U.S. Steel--the largest steel company--was adopted by other steel companies (Ulman 1962:70).

However, the industry won this more centralized, formalized, and predictable relationship by conceding a certain amount of autonomy to local union leaders.   To appease leaders of the growing autonomy movement and provide greater stability in union:management relations, local unions were guaranteed limited control over shopfloor working conditions. In 1947, USWA negotiators won a clause in the steel industry master agreement which prevented management in some companies from changing existing shopfloor arrangements without local union approval.   "Section 2B" on "Local Working Conditions" covered matters such as crew size, relief arrangements, seniority districts, work scheduling, wash-up time, coffee breaks and check-in arrangements.* This provided local union representatives and rank-and-file steelworkers with considerable protection from subsequent management pressures to change work practices.   It also gave them shopfloor leverage to influence management policies in newly constructed workplaces; the union could grant concessions in old areas in a tradeoff for protection of certain worker rights in new areas.

In terms of wages and benefits, significant gains were made in the 1950s. Figure 3.1 shows the significant increases in real wages during this period.   In 1955, the union won a 52-week supplemental unemployment benefit plan for workers with more than two years' seniority.   This guaranteed workers almost full wages during layoff periods.   In the same contract negotiations, the union won a cost-of-living escalator and increased wages (Betheil 1978:4).   This settlement pushed steelworkers' wages ahead of other manufacturing

---

* The clause prevented changes in local union practices "as long as the employees involved wished them to remain in effect or until the production processes forming the 'basis' of such practices remained unchanged" (Ulman 1962:79).   This later qualification was interpreted to mean the introduction of new technology (Betheil 1978:4-5).

employees--even unionized industrial workers, such as automobile workers who had been paid wages on par with steel (ibid.). At the same time, this agreement further rationalized industrial relations in steel. Before 1955, contracts contained provisions subject to annual negotiations over wage reopeners; these were eliminated. Industry could better predict labor costs and avoid disruptive strikes.

UNION LEADERSHIP CENTRALIZATION

With the 1947 contract provision giving limited workplace autonomy to local unionists and with the significant wage and benefit improvements in the 1955 contract, International union leaders shielded themselves from rank-and-file criticism. Any dissidence that did exist was focused on the local workplace. This gave International leaders the opportunity to further consolidate their control over industrywide bargaining, union conventions, finances, staff, committees, and district leadership. For example, at the 1950 Convention, the International leadership was made the sole "contracting party" in all collective agreements (United Steelworkers of America 1950:288). This not only boxed out a specific role for local union officials in collective bargaining, but it eliminated the discretion that District Directors had employed in interpreting contract language during the life of contract agreements. It effectively stripped the Directors of their most important decision-making power (Ulman 1962:70). Through the 1950s, top officers succeeded in moving control in collective bargaining to smaller negotiating committees over which they could exert direct control.

In other union decision-making bodies, the International tightened its control. By using its control over the information delegates received as well as its own role in chairing the conventions, the International leadership dominated local union delegates at Wage Policy Committee meetings and Conventions--two bodies supposed to give USWA members a voice in negotiations and general policy-making. Local union delegates at such meetings found it increasingly difficult to organize their disparate interests in opposition to the centralized International control (ibid.:51-68).

The International leadership also gained tight control over finances. First, it gained control as a result of dues "check off" systems. These were mechanisms established throughout the 1940s that allowed union dues to be deducted directly from workers' pay checks and sent directly to the International Secretary-Treasurer without going through the local union. Second, by using its right to take control of local union administration in the event of "questionable" financial (or political) practices, the International leadership wielded a powerful organizational weapon (ibid.:40-41). Third, the International leadership's domination of Constitutional Conventions allowed it to win dues increases despite considerable membership opposition (there were three dues increases in the period between 1948 and 1956). This helped to build up a substantial treasury--much of which could be used at the International leadership's discretion.

Changes in the character of union membership also facilitated increased International leadership dominance. Diversification of the membership's occupational and industrial characteristics made it increasingly difficult for local rank-and-file groups to understand and react to the interests of all members. By 1957, the USWA held contracts in 38 major Standard Industrial Classification groups; less than half of the union membership was in primary metals (ibid.:43). This diversification process--which sped up in the 1960s and 1970s--gave top union officials a political advantage over local union members. International leaders had the vantage point with which to view--and the administrative network with which to control--the diverse membership. Local union leaders did not have this overview or control. It is no coincidence that during this period the union staff--appointed by the International leadership--played an increasingly important role in union affairs ranging from advising local unions on administrative matters to participating in industry-wide contract negotiations. Thus, changes in the union's formal and informal organizational structures--precipitated by changes in the social and economic environment during the 1947-59 period--facilitated the growth of the International leadership's power over the organization.

THE INTERNATIONAL UNION LEADERSHIP'S "BASES OF INFLUENCE"

Using existing sociological models of influence in organizations as an analytical tool, one can see how the various organizational changes in the union increased the International's power in the 1950s. In *Organizational Design*, Jeffrey Pfeffer outlines four "bases for influence" that leaders can use in their control over the organization:

> 1) the possession of or ability to control critical resources, 2) the control of or access to information and information channels, 3) legitimacy of the desired position or actions, and 4) formal authority, as derived from the formally designated organizational structure and constitution [1978:198].

The USWA International leadership's central role in collecting and distributing funds as well as their success in building up the central union treasury through dues increases strengthened their influence on the first basis. Their ability to concentrate decision-making--particularly in collective bargaining functions--into small organizational bodies which they regulated gave them control over internal union

communications.   Moreover,   diversification   of   the
membership--with the concomitant increase in geographical
distance between members and in divergence of interests among
members--enhanced the influence of International officers.

Over the same period of time the "legitimacy" of top
USWA leaders increased.   One can interpret "legitimacy" to
mean the perception among rank-and-file members that union
leaders have a right to control decision making.   (Pfeffer
defines "legitimacy" as "a perceived congruence between social
values and organizational products and actions" [1978:159].)
The argument presented by Steelworker officials (along with
other American union officials) that unions need to centralize
their structures to "match" the centralization of industry did
have credibility in the eyes of many rank-and-file workers.
Increased concentration of industrial control in the whole
economy served to legitimate centralization of union functions.

Finally, in looking at the last "basis of influence"--formal
control over the organization--it is obvious that the USWA
leadership had much of this from the first days of the union.
Although the International did make a few constitutional
changes, they always had a strong formal organizational
foundation for their power.   However, the major argument
being made here is that it was the changing social
environment--in particular the state of the industry and the
union leadership's relationship to that industry--that allowed
the union leadership to *realize the power* sanctioned by formal
structures.   The mere existence of formal organizational
structures does not mean that centralization will exist.
Rather, the social, political, and economic environments in
which the organization functions serve to bring about the
actual centralization.

THE RANK AND FILE MOVEMENT: STILL DECENTRALIZED

Despite centralization of union administration during this
period, the rank-and-file movement remained decentralized.
The "national" reform organization that did emerge in the
mid-1950s was merely a loose coalition of informal local union
networks.   As a result of the concessions made to local
autonomists in the late 1940s, grassroots activity had focused
on local issues.   Local caucuses changed little during this
period; issues and strategies of the early 1950s were the same
as those used in the 1940s.   The movement remained an
informal, loosely tied network of local activists.   There was no
attempt to establish more formal insurgent organizations on a
local level, nor was there an effort to reach out and establish
a unionwide organization.

"Section 2B" had allowed rank-and-filers some sense of
control over the workplace and had dulled rank-and-file
criticism of incumbent union officials.   The International also
"managed" militancy by turning it on during contract
negotiations and by turning it off after settlements were

reached.   The   International   warmed   up   grassroots anti-company sentiment at negotiation time--in union newspaper articles, speeches at conferences, and messages to local union meetings.   In contract talks, top union leaders could threaten the industry by saying it would let local militants loose if the industry did not agree to union demands.   Indeed, the strikes called by USWA leaders throughout the '50s did tap local militancy.   Not only did it put pressure on the companies, but it served as a catharsis for local union militants.   It maintained an image of an adversarial relationship with the industry, and allowed the rank and file to let off steam.* Thus one factor that inhibited growth of rank-and-file organizations beyond the local level was the toleration of--and occasional stimulation of--militancy.   Secondly, with "Section 2B" in place,   there   was   a   real   role   for   local   unions   in union:management relations.   With opportunties for input at local levels, the incentive for building a union-wide grassroots movement was reduced.

A Focus on "Union Democracy"

When a unionwide rank-and-file reform organization did emerge in the mid-1950s, it did not focus on workplace or wage   issues.   Rather   it   grew   out   of   concern   over administrative centralization in the union.   Specifically, a small rank-and-file insurgent organization was established after the third   dues   increase   in   eight   years   was   passed   by   a Constitutional   Convention   heavily   influenced   by   the International leadership.   The new movement had a difficult time organizing support because few local grassroots networks were   present   during   this   period.   Moreover,   because   the dominant orientation of those dissident organizations that did exist was on local issues and local organizing, dissidents lacked the skills and resources needed to develop a successful anti-International campaign at the international level.   The following section analyzes the emergence and ultimate failure of the Dues Protest Committee (DPC) of the mid-1950s.   However, despite   its   underdeveloped   organizational   structure   and strategy, the DPC represented a changing consciousness among rank-and-file activists, i.e. a consciousness that there was a need to build a unionwide organization if changes were to be made in the USWA.

---

* This function is not unique to the Steelworkers union.   In his study of the United Auto Workers, William Serrin (1974) found a similar union leadership approach to turning on and off worker militancy.

The Dues Protest Movement: A Weak Unionwide Organization

The first rank-and-file electoral challenge to the International leadership occurred in 1956, when the Dues Protest Committee built an organized opposition to the top union administration.[2] Ostensibly formed as a protest to a dues increase at the 1956 Los Angeles Constitutional Convention, the DPC gained strength by pursuing issues related to union democracy, leadership accountability to the membership, honesty in elections, protection of local union autonomy, and better shopfloor union representation. The national rank-and-file organization was formally established at an October 1956, McKeesport, Pennsylvania meeting attended by 50 Pittsburgh-area Steelworkers. Initial recruitment of DPC supporters centered around a petition and local resolution campaign calling for a special dues roll-back convention.[3] Most support came from the large industrial steel producing areas--particularly from the Western Pennsylania and Eastern Ohio industrial region (Tomko; *Fortune* 1957).

The Dues Protest Committee was loosely organized. It had no formal structure, rather it was run by a network of activists concentrated in a few basic steel locals. The DPC had no formal mechanisms for rank-and-file input. Although DPC leaders felt that they had "good solid grassroots involvement," the organization was weak outside its Western Pennsylvania and Northeastern Ohio home ground (Piccirilli). Only limited campaign activity was done in industrial centers in the Midwest, South, and West (Peurala; Wright). Because the Midwest and Western regions were areas into which the steel industry had expanded in the period immediately after World War II, this limitation reduced the movement's contact with the growing union membership in these areas.

The absence of significant numbers of local union insurgent organizations hampered the campaign. Ed Mann, a campaigner for the Committee, remarks that organizing had to be done "from scratch." He observes that local support did not come from groups, but rather from previously unconnected union members "with common interests" (Mann). Without the intermediate mechanisms--local and regional rank-and-file organizations--the DPC was faced with the massive task of reaching each union member directly.

The DPC was also up against an International administration with considerably greater organizational resources. The insurgent organization did not have access to the International directory of locals; they had to rely on their limited contacts, supplemented by telephone-book listings, to construct a partial list of the large local unions. Also, the challengers had nothing equivalent to the hundreds of full-time staff representatives that the incumbent administration could use in campaigning in the thousands of USWA locals.

It should also be noted that in the mid-1950s, McCarthyism was still very much alive. Many local dissidents had been prohibited from holding union office in the early 1950s just because they were accused of being communists. One of the reasons for the lack of local grassroots organizations was the dampening effect that anti-communism had had on the formation of political opposition groups in union locals. Ed Mann comments that "the McCarthy days of the 1950s killed everything that even looked like an independent [organization]; anybody who got two people together was immediately red-baited or run out" (Mann). John Barbero, who was later elected vice-president of Local 1462 in Youngstown, also recalls that dissidents were "red-baited" during the 1950s. Conservative union leaders used anti-communism as a license to squelch dissent. Barbero remembers that during this period, administration critics were routinely called out of order at meetings. He adds that no matter what issues dissidents raised at local union meetings, the local union president "had such a well-organized machine that it was 'sit down and shut up.' He had the goons in the hall to enforce it. An opposition candidate who asked for the right to speak would be thrown out on the floor" (*Ramparts* 1972:22). During some local union elections, companies even "red-baited" union militants in literature that they distributed to employees (J. Balanoff). Combined with the International leadership's administrative power and the DPC's internal organizational weaknesses, anti-communism helped to undermine the only unionwide insurgent movement of the mid-1950s.

Electoral Defeat

The DPC candidates lost by a margin of 2:1. The International administration subsequently made reprisals against locals backing the insurgent candidates, e.g. imposing administratorships on their locals and attempting to suspend DPC leaders from union membership (Hardman 1972; Herling 1972; Ulman 1962). However, while such harassment did weaken the insurgent movement, it was the movement's own weak, loosely organized character that undermined any emergence of a successful grassoots insurgent in the late 1950s. DPC members did regroup for the 1961 International election under the name "Organization for Membership Rights" (OMR). Using criticism of the recently signed 1959 basic steel contract, they attempted to rally anti-International sentiment behind OMR. However, once again, poor internal organization and an underdeveloped local union network reduced their effectiveness. OMR died without collecting nominations for any candidate in the 1961 elections (Litch).

CONCLUSIONS

The rank-and-file movement of the 1950s and the specific organizations that emerged out of it were molded by a set of social structures and economic conditions unique to the 1950s. Industrial prosperity provided steel companies with an economic surplus with which to "buy" industrial peace. At the same time, it gave the International union leadership the grace period during which it could consolidate its control over the union. It was the combination of prosperity, industry pressure for expansion, and further industry centralization that produced an environment in which the union felt pressured to further centralize its functions. In this environment, top union leaders transformed what had been mere "formal" control over the organization into real control over the "bases of influence" in the union. When grassroots opposition to union centralization did finally emerge, it not only faced the obstacles of an immature movement with limited expertise in organizational strategies, but it was also up against a centralized International union leadership more powerful than the one which had existed in earlier years.

After the DPC was defeated, the steel industry put increased pressure on the International leadership to further consolidate its control over the bargaining process. The steel industry had enjoyed prosperity through the 1950s, but was coming out of a recession in 1958. By centralizing collective bargaining, it helped to insulate negotiations from local activists, who continued to guard their control over workplace relations protected by "2B" and to press for wage and benefit improvements. This would guarantee the industry a more predictable relationship with the union; the industry would be able to deal with a centralized International leadership rather than with a large number of more militant local union leaders. As will be shown in the next chapter, the 1959 contract settlement and early 1960s contracts brought about significant changes in the relationship between the union, the industry, and the union membership. Within the rank-and-file movement national issues became increasingly important. Dissidents started to focus more on the union's relationship to the industry, rather than just on organizational "democracy." Although the development of a strategy for unionwide organizing continued to be problematic for the rank-and-file movement, the movement increasingly paid attention to decisions made at unionwide levels.

Chapter 4

Industrial Reorganization and Union Centralization
1959–1973

Although many issues contributing to rank-and-file disenchantment with the union became clearer in the 1960s, e.g. lack of real wage increases, job loss, and centralization of decision making, became clearer in the 1960s, structural changes in the industry and the union made organizing for change more difficult. Union policy was increasingly made at top levels. The rank-and-file movement, still consisting of relatively autonomous local networks, did not quickly adapt its strategies to the new political environment. Throughout the 1960s, the movement was still oriented toward local organizing; attempts to use local strategies in developing unionwide support ended in failure. Before analyzing changes in the union and the rank-and-file movement, it is important to examine changes in the industry that affected both the issues facing steelworkers and the organizational and economic environment in which union politics took place.

THE INDUSTRY

The 1960s represent a watershed decade for the American steel industry. Faced with rapidly deteriorating plants and outdated technology, the American industry was under pressure to reorganize if it was to survive. Much of the pressure was the result of its weakness in sales on the foreign market and the encroachment of foreign steel in the American market. As Table 4.1 shows, steel imports increased significantly in the late 1950s and early 1960s. In a related trend, the U.S. share of world steel production also declined (see Fig. 4.1). The U.S. industry found it increasingly difficult to undersell foreign steel companies which had newer and more efficient plants.

The encroachment of imports upon the American market was directly related to both a worldwide drop in the costs of raw materials--particularly iron ore and coal--and to reduced shipping costs (Crandall 1981:34-35). The U.S. industry had previously had an advantage over foreign competitors because of its access to relatively cheap nearby raw materials and lower transportation costs due to its obvious proximity to the American market. These advantages more than compensated for America's relatively high labor costs compared to other countries. However, after 1958, when worldwide materials and transportation costs (particularly shipping) declined, the relatively high U.S. labor costs became more of a liability.

This change in costs is apparent when one compares U.S. costs to the costs of its most formidable foreign competitor--Japan. Because most of its steel mills were destroyed in World War II, Japan rebuilt its industry in the 1940s and 1950s, using newer and more efficient equipment. As shown in Table 4.2, before the 1958 shift in worldwide raw material prices, U.S. costs were significantly lower than Japanese costs. Moreover, since materials represented more than 75 percent of Japanese production costs and approximately 50 percent of U.S. production costs, the difference in raw materials costs had significant consequences for prices (ibid.:48). However, in the 1960s, after the worldwide decline in raw material prices, the ratio of Japanese to American material costs was reversed. During the same years, the labor cost ratio remained constant or changed in favor of Japan. This ultimately affected sections of the U.S. steel market, particularly "price-sensitive products" such as hot rolled steel, cold rolled steel, bars, plate, and structurals. By 1962, for all of these products, foreign steel import prices were below American prices even after freight costs were included. (There was a temporary reversal of this trend between 1973 and 1975, due in part to the energy crisis, but by 1976 the pre-1973 cost differences returned [ibid.:49].) This foreign competition put tremendous pressure on the U.S. industry to protect the remaining sections of its market. The industry and union lobbied for import restrictions.

However, steel industry action to protect its fiscal health involved more than lobbying for import controls. First, the industry embarked on a program to introduce new technology into American mills at a faster pace. Second, steel companies looked outside of the steel industry for new investment opportunities and new sources of profit. Third, the industry followed industrial relations policies that would hold down labor costs and increase labor productivity.

New Technology

Significant increases in capital expenditures in steel production were apparent in the period 1964 to 1970 (see Table 4.3). This reflects the introduction of new technology in the industry. It also reflects the availability of newly found revenue--partly from reduced labor costs (discussed later) and from increased demand during the peak Vietnam War years, 1964-70. The technology introduced included more productive, labor-saving machinery which gave management greater control over the workplace. The changes initiated in the 1960s--primarily increased use of the Basic Oxygen Furnace (BOF), continuous casting process, and computer-controlled production--ultimately changed the shape of steelmaking in the 1970s and 1980s.

To understand where the technological changes were introduced, a simple understanding of the basic stages of steel production is helpful. Steel mill production can be divided into two basic processes: (1) raw steel production and (2) the transformation of raw steel into more usable forms, e.g. rolled sheets for automobile manufacturing or I-beams for building construction. The technological innovations of the 1960s affected both of these processes. In raw steel production the Basic Oxygen Furnace (BOF) replaced aging Open Hearth Furnaces. Compared to an Open Hearth Furnace, the BOF produces more steel at a higher quality with fewer workers in a shorter period of time. As shown in Table 4.4, in the 1960s, there was a significant shift from the labor-intensive open hearth to the less labor-intensive BOF.

Changes in technologies involved in the shaping of steel into various forms, e.g. I-beams, rails, rods, and sheets, were also made. "Continuous casting" was introduced into many mills during the 1960s. This process allows steel shapes to be cast directly from molten steel; it saves energy, labor, and in-plant transportation time. Like the BOF, the continuous caster was significantly less labor intensive than its technological predecessor. In fact, the U.S. Department of Labor (1975:23) indicated that 10 to 15 percent less manpower is required in continuous casting than in ingot casting. The increased importance of continuous casting in U.S. steel production since the 1960s is shown in Table 4.5.

The third major technological innovation first introduced in the 1960s is the computerized rolling mill. This has been developed more slowly than the other two technologies, and it is still not thoroughly implemented in American mills. However, computer technology promises to have a lasting impact on the workplace. In a rolling mill where a number of skilled workers--usually union members--might have controlled the speed and quality of steel coming off the rolls, a single computer operator can now coordinate the same process. In some mills computer operators are non-union salaried employees.

Compared to previous workplace arrangements, workers in a computerized mill (other than the computer operator) have less control over their work, i.e. pace, tasks, and judgment in eliminating problems. For example, in another area of the plant away from the actual production lines, a crane operator who occupied a job with a considerable degree of worker discretion over speed of work is more subject to computer-determined speed in a modern mill. In some mills crane operators are directly given "orders" by the computer. A steel mill computer consultant describes such a mill: "Each time the crane man performs an operation...he pushes a button that says: 'Okay, I've done that job. Now what do you want me to do?'" (McManus 1979:MP7). The computerization trend started in the 1960s is likely to continue, changing work relations in all parts of the steel mill:

> Hierarchy computer control is the new buzz word. This calls for computerizing all the data functions of steel production--order entry, order tracking, inventory control, production- scheduling, and so forth.
>
> The computers are arranged in a pyramid that resembles a plant organization chart. The process computers are on one level. Supervisory computers are on one or more tiers. At the top is the big management, or host, computer [ibid.:MP3].

As noted above, these technological innovations were part of a broader trend in the U.S. steel industry to increase efficiency. In the 1959-1980 period, this involved phasing out inefficient mills, shutting down entire plants, and updating the equipment in the remaining mills.* Production *capacity* was not substantially increased by these investments. Unlike the 1950s when the post-war capacity of less than 100 million was

---

* A "mill" is a production unit within a larger integrated steel complex or "plant." A mill may have a workforce of a few hundred, while an integrated plant typically has a workforce of a few thousand.

increased by almost 50 percent by 1959 (U.S. General Accounting Office 1981;2-15), capacity increased by only 13 million tons between 1959 and 1969, and 3.2 million tons between 1969 and 1978 (Crandall 1981:Table 2-4). Only one new integrated mill was constructed in the 1960s and 1970s; Bethlehem Steel's Burns Harbor, Indiana plant, opened in 1968. However, as shown in Table 4.6, *labor productivity* (output per man-hour--which primarily measures the combined effect of labor and capital productivity) has increased appreciably since the late 1950s. Much of this increase can be attributed to introduction of new technology and the shutdown of inefficient plants.

Diversification

Starting in the 1960s and continuing into the 1980s, a number of steel companies developed diversification programs. In the late 1960s, U.S. Steel modified its corporate structure to facilitate this process.[1] Inland and Armco also began diversifying primarily into the chemical industries (although Inland's investments have been somewhat modest). National Steel became joint owner of a large primary aluminum producer. Still other companies merged with or were taken over by non-steel concerns. In the late 1960s, Youngstown Sheet and Tube merged with Lykes Corporation--a shipping concern--while Jones and Laughlin was taken over by Ling-Temco-Vought--another conglomerate. Smaller companies were also taken over: Colt Industries took over Crucible Steel, NVF acquired Sharon Steel, and Athlone Industries took over Jessup Steel. As would become apparent in the late 1970s, the function of these takeovers by non-steel companies was to use profits from steel in expanding segments of the non-steel operations. Little was reinvested in steel mills, guaranteeing that mills would become obsolete and close--as they did in the late 1970s. According to researchers for the Ohio Public Interest Campaign, the conglomerates' interest in buying steel companies

> was sparked by two factors: 1) the large cash flow of steel companies, mainly caused by depreciation and other write-offs, and 2) the low prices of steel companies' stock. These two factors meant that large supplies of cash could be acquired very cheaply [Kelly & Shutes 1979:38].

Kelly and Shutes quoted *Business Week* to the effect that "the conglomerateurs' steel acquisitions were seen as cash boxes for corporate growth in other areas" (ibid.).

IMPACT ON WORKERS, THE UNION AND LABOR RELATIONS

The industry's modernization and reorganization profoundly affected steelworkers, as well as the USWA itself. In the long run the industry's program of automation, diversification, and contraction of steel production reduced the power of labor in the industry. By increasing its day-to-day control over the workers on the shopfloor, automation gave management more control over the production process. Diversification out of steel and contraction of steel production increased the companies' capacity to weather a strike because steel revenues no longer represented such a large proportion of total corporate income. However, since the reorganization only started in the 1960s and was far from complete until the 1980s, the industry was both (1) concerned with stabilizing wages in order to fuel capital investment and eliminate part of its disadvantage in competing with foreign companies with lower labor costs and (2) concerned with warding off any labor unrest at this crucial period. Therefore, to hold down its costs and generate enough capital to fuel its modernization and reorganization, the industry sought more predictable and "cooperative" labor relations during this period. The industry redoubled its efforts to pressure the union to centralize its bargaining functions. International union leaders were receptive to this, since it further consolidated their power over the union--particularly in the wake of the recent electoral challenges to incumbent International union officials.

Centralized Bargaining

In the contract settlement after the 1959 strike, local union control over negotiations and workplace practices was reduced through the creation of the Human Relations Committee (HRC), composed of International union officials and company representatives. This became the primary forum in contract negotiations in the early 1960s and supplanted the Wage Policy Committee--a body comprised of local union representatives--which had played a strong role in past bargaining sessions (Herling 1972:99). One measure of the loss of local influence in contract bargaining was the HRC's elimination of "Section 2B" protection of local work rules.[2] The relationship between the International union and the industry had become a cooperative one. The adversarial and institutionalized adversarial relationships of the first two periods (1936-47 and 1947-59) had disappeared. No major strikes occurred during this period.

Stabilized Real Wages and Declining Employment

The real wage increases that steelworkers had been getting in contract settlements prior to the 1960s did not continue into the new decade.   Real wages stabilized during this period (see Figure 4.1).   Whereas steelworkers' real wages had increased by 62.8 percent in the 12 years from 1947 to 1959 (a 5.2 percent annual average increase), they increased by only 16.0 percent in the 13 years from 1959 to 1972 (a 1.2 percent annual average increase).   In the first period steelworkers were way ahead of the 37.9 percent increase in real wages among all manufacturing industry workers, while in the second period they fell behind the 21.5 percent increase among workers in the broader category (U.S. Department of Labor 1979).   These differences are also shown in Figure 4.1.   After 1958, the number of production jobs in the steel industry never again reached the 600,000 level achieved in earlier years (see Fig. 4.2).   While employment fluctuated in the '60s, it ultimately was leading to a decline in the '70s.   Through job and wage stabilization, steelworkers were subsidizing reorganization of the industry.

The reorganization entailed more automation, increased management control in the workplace, and a reduction in the size of the steel workforce.   The anticipation of technological changes discussed earlier in this chapter was undoubtedly a key reason for the steel industry's successful push to drop Section 2B and centralize steel bargaining.   The Basic Oxygen Furnace, continuous casting, and computer-controlled rolling mills sped up production, reduced labor needs, and increased management's control over the workplace--all changes likely to be resisted by rank-and-file workers.

THE RANK-AND-FILE MOVEMENT

Worker dissatisfaction in reaction to job reductions, declines in workplace control, and greater union centralization became increasingly apparent during this period.   However at the same time, the nature of rank-and-file opposition was shaped by these changes.   Deprived of local union mechanisms with which to affect wages and working conditions--mechanisms which had existed prior to 1960--local dissidents were forced to look to regional and international levels for airing their grievances within the union.   This was already apparent with the formation of the Dues Protest Committee in 1956 and the short-lived Organization for Membership Rights in 1961. However, despite the recognition by rank-and-file dissidents that there had been increased concentration of policy-making power at top levels of the union, few adjustments were made in dissidents' strategies.   Rank-and-file dissidents did not undertake the formidable task of developing local rank-and-file organizations that ultimately could join into a unionwide organization (Herling 1972:56; Litch).

This is not to say that grassroots disenchantment did not exist. The initial effects of real wage stabilization in the 1960s, after decades of real wage increases, along with deteriorating working conditions and reduced input into union policy making, spurred on rank-and-file critics in the early 1960s. Steelworkers had lost ground in wages and working conditions largely because of "weak" contract settlements in 1962 and 1963. The *Wall Street Journal* called the 1963 contract "the lowest cost settlement since 1944 (Herling 1972:98,99). The settlement upset local union officers so much that following the 1963 agreement, all local presidents representing Pittsburgh Steel and Jones and Laughlin plants refused to sign the pact. Over one-half of the officers representing Republic Steel employees followed suit (ibid.:174; Radovich).

Despite a generalized local sentiment for a change in the International leadership, there were no signs of an emergence of any unionwide rank-and-file organization able to affect change at top union levels where the power now rested. An organization of Black USWA members critical of the USWA International leadership's failure to appoint Blacks to staff positions did emerge at this time. However, as shown elsewhere, this organization--the Ad Hoc Committee of Concerned Black Steelworkers--was quickly coopted by the International leadership. Ad Hoc never represented a large cross-section of union members--even Black union members (Nyden 1983).

Given the existence of disenchantment in the absence of any grassroots organization, it is not surprising that the next electoral challenger to the incumbent USWA president came from *within* the top ranks. In 1965, in what has been called a "palace coup," International Secretary-Treasurer I.W. Abel successfully ran against incumbent David McDonald for the USWA presidency. Unlike the OMC or DPC, Abel was able to organize grassroots support by using his position as an International officer.* With the help of International staff representatives and a number of friendly incumbent District Directors, Abel used the International structure as a means of organizing rank-and-file dissidents for his purposes. (The "International Committee to Elect Abel-Burke-Molony" was composed mainly of USWA staff persons, district directors, and professional campaigners from other sectors of the labor movement.) Access to official union structures was the key political resource available to Abel which was not available to grassroots-based movements.

---

* The Abel-McDonald campaign is examined closely in Herling (1972). It will be discussed here only insofar as it provides an understanding of the development (or underdevelopment) of the rank-and-file movement in the USWA.

Just as Abel mobilized the International union organization to pull together grassroots support for his candidacy, he mobilized the union organization to consolidate his power and insulate the International leadership from the rank and file. Union members who accepted Abel's campaign promise of "return the union to its members" were quickly disillusioned once "their" candidate took office. Collective bargaining remained centralized; Constitutional Convention structures were not altered to facilitate a stronger voice by rank-and-file union members; and the power of International staff representatives over District and local union affairs was not reduced. To put it succinctly, centralization of decision-making was not altered.

The Abel victory was a change in personal leadership styles rather than an introduction of administrative reforms. Although the change of faces in the International office did serve to calm rank-and-file dissidence for a short period, the major social and economic elements that had precipitated grassroots disenchantment remained. The continued absence of real wage increases, combined with the layoff of 65,000 union members in the last half of the '60s, produced an environment conducive for the development of renewed grassroots insurgency (Herling 1972:367-69).

In the late 1960s, the organizers of the DPC and OMR recruited some new supporters, and regrouped under the name Rank and File Team (RAFT). As it became apparent that the reshuffling of International officials was not making any difference in wages and working conditions, support for a rank-and-file reform organization grew once again. However, like its predecessors, RAFT was not a unionwide organization. It was concentrated in Ohio--particularly in the Youngstown area. It did have some contacts with individual unionists outside the area, but these were limited primarily to Pittsburgh and Chicago. RAFT relied heavily on the rank-and-file's familiarity with their candidates' names rather than relying on any reform program. Because of this, the death of their candidate--Donald Rarick, the DPC's 1956 candidate--prior to the nominating period hurt the campaign. Only RAFT's International Secretary-Treasurer candidate, Morros Brummitt, received sufficient nominations to get on the ballot.

Subsequently, RAFT decided to join with Emile Narick, an assistant general counsel for the USWA who had already won enough nominations to appear as a presidential candidate on the ballot. Narrick used his position as International staff representative to gain access to potential supporters in union locals (Litch). Narick lost the 1969 election, but polled 40 percent of the vote--a a surprisingly high percentage, given that he was relatively unknown and had a weak campaign organization. Nevertheless once again this indirectly pointed out the organizational weakness of the rank-and-file movement.

If a relative unknown without a broad-based campaign organization could do so well in an election, it seems that a candidate sponsored by a well-organized grassroots reform organization could have won the election. Grassroots dissidence was present, but the rank-and-file movement appeared incapable of using it to bolster its political strength at the International union level. Because of the underdevelopment of local union dissident caucuses and their inability to establish a unionwide support network, DPC, OMR, and RAFT had failed to garner enough support to achieve electoral victory. However, despite the apparent weakness of local union reform organizations in the 1960s, changes were occurring at the local level.

CHANGES IN THE LOCAL 1010 RANK-AND-FILE CAUCUS

Continuing the examination of the Local 1010 Rank-and-File Caucus as a case study of changing goals and structure of local dissident networks, one can see significant alterations in the 1960s. The personal leadership style, informal organizational structure, and exclusively local orientation that had characterized the Caucus throughout much of the 1950s had disappeared. The Caucus adopted a more formal organizational structure and set its sights on International as well as local issues. Although ostensibly this was attributed to the "style" of a new Caucus leader, Jim Balanoff, it was actually the movement's response to the changes in the workplace and the union, as well as a reaction to changes in the overall economy.

By the 1960s, the International's presence was strongly felt at the local union level--in collective bargaining and in union policies affecting local administration. A reform caucus could not help but address unionwide issues; the day of an autonomist ideology was past. Under the centralized bargaining process which reduced local input, real wage increases were not made, and the workplace control of the 1950s was lost. This made local activists very aware of the importance of organizing and addressing issues at the unionwide level.

Also, to build such organizations, a larger, more committed, local membership was needed. A few local progressive activists were no match for conservative local leaders who were backed by the International. The International was now more aggressive in consolidating its control over the local unions--unlike the International in the late 1940s and early 1950s, when it was more willing to concede some local autonomy for internal organizational harmony. Only grassroots organizations capable of winning the support of broad networks of workers on the shopfloor could survive in this new environment. Weak, small, personally led organizations tended to disintegrate. Broader-based, better-organized groups were more likely to survive.

The Local 1010 Caucus that emerged in the late 1960s and early 1970s was an expanded one with a tighter structure. In addition to regular meetings, elected offices were created, regular internal elections held, and essential organizational functions formally coordinated, e.g. finances, newsletter publication, and record-keeping. During election campaigns, the Caucus rented a storefront near the mill to give the organization a more permanent appearance. It initiated more ongoing activities not directly related to specific election campaigns. "Educational meetings," where a labor historian spoke or a labor history film was shown, were held at the Caucus headquarters. The Caucus sponsored dinners and picnics to encourage involvement.

Caucus membership grew in this period; compared to the six or seven active leaders of the 1950s, the Caucus now had ten or fifteen active leaders and the capability of mobilizing fifty or more union members to attend important Caucus meetings. This tighter organization was a more effective net in catching shopfloor workers who were disenchanted with the union, working conditions, or wage levels. Thus, at this time, the growth of local caucuses was a function of rising grassroots disenchantment *and* more effective organizational nets.

CONCLUSIONS

The steel industry prosperity of the 1950s disappeared in the 1960s. Major American integrated steel producers were under pressure to restructure production in the face of increased competition. They could not afford to grant real wage increases or to continue even limited workers' shopfloor control. Responding to industry pressure, union leaders accepted real wage stabilization and gave up some local control. At the same time, top USWA leaders sought to protect themselves by gaining a tighter grip over union decision making. From the point of view of rank-and-file steelworkers, the 1960s represented a period of relative austerity and declining power. Union centralization, stabilized wages, and diminished local control over working conditions combined to increase grassroots disenchantment with union and industry policy. However, this unrest was not articulated; no unionwide rank-and-file reform organization gained strength in the 1960s. Not until the early 1970s did such a movement emerge in the union.

Chapter 5

Rise of the Rank-and-File
Movement *1973–1979*

In the first half of the 1970s, steelworker disenchantment over wages, working conditions, and union leader responsiveness to the membership continued to increase. The emergence of new rank-and-file reform organizations in some union locals, the expansion of the size of already-existing reform caucuses in other union locals, and the electoral success of these caucuses were foreboding signals to both industry and International union leadership. The industry, not having fully achieved its reorganization, could not afford major labor conflict at this time. The International union, still sensitive to political rumblings in its basic steel locals--which still represented almost 50 percent of its membership in 1970--could not afford to ignore the growing grassroots movement. Thus, both the industry and International union sought a way to cool dissidence. It was at this time that the Experimental Negotiating Agreement (ENA) was established by the steel industry negotiating committee and the USWA

International leadership. The substantial increases in real wages set by the Agreement ended the real wage stabilization of the 1960s. At the same time, it prohibited the union from striking at contract expiry and committed both parties to arbitration if an agreement was not reached by a set date. Thus, the ENA bought time for both the industry and the union in their respective consolidations of power. It was in this social climate that the rank-and-file movement grew.

The next two chapters will examine the rise of the rank-and-file movement in the 1970s. In addition to examining the impact of industrial and union structure on the movement, the political strategies and organizational structure of the most prominent rank-and-file reform organization--Steelworkers Fight Back--will be analyzed.

THE INDUSTRY

In many ways the 1970s represent a pivotal decade for the American steel industry. Many structural changes that were apparent but underdeveloped in the early 1970s, were well established by the end of the decade. In 1970, the industry was still quite vulnerable to labor conflict in basic steel; by the end of the decade it was much less vulnerable. By 1979, the character of the American steel industry had changed in four fundamental ways: (1) efficiency or productivity of the industry had improved as a result of the introduction of new technology and the phase out of outdated mills and plants, (2) there was an apparent forfeiture of a proportion of the American market to foreign steel producers, (3) smaller non-integrated steel companies, also called mini-mills, had increased their share of the domestic market,* and (4) larger integrated producers, while accounting for a smaller share of the market, had embarked on diversification plans, abandoning steel production for other industrial investments;

As shown in the previous chapter, the impact of new technologies introduced in the 1960s--the BOF, continuous casters, and computer-controlled mills--was ultimately felt in the 1970s. To the BOF and electric furnaces, which accounted for 12 percent of U.S. steel production in 1964, accounted for more than 60 percent of the steel produced in 1980 (this was shown in Table 4.4). Similarly, only 2.9 percent of steel was continously cast in 1969 compared to 20.3 percent in 1980 (as shown in Table 4.5). New mill construction completed in the

---

* An integrated producer is engaged in all processes in the steel production cycle from raw steel production to finishing. A non-integrated producer is not involved in all phases of steel production, e.g. it may have a rolling mill supplied with steel from an integrated producer or from melting down scrap in an electric furnace. The product line of a non-integrated producer is also usually specialized.

1970s also introduced computer-controlled equipment. In the early 1970s, as the industry was completing its modernization program, the industry was quite vulnerable to labor pressures. It is not coincidental that this was a period of reconciliation between company and union.

However, at the same time as industrial peace existed, the structure of the industry was changing in a fundamental way which ultimately undercut the power of steelworkers vis-a-vis the industry. Automation and labor force contraction in integrated steel plants gave producers more control over the workplace. Also, the encroachment of foreign steel products on the American market--discussed in the previous chapter--continued during this period. This reduced demand for domestic steel, reduced the basic steel labor force, and undercut union membership. In addition to this, integrated steel producers were facing competition from a new source--non-integrated mini-mills. These mills not only took business away from the larger steel companies, but since they are generally non-union, the union's leverage over wages and labor relations in the steel industry was further undermined. The growth of domestic non-integrated producers is discussed next.

Growth of Non-integrated Producers.

Unlike integrated producers, non-integrated steel producers or mini-mills do not incorporate all phases of the steel production process in their plants. Generally they do not include production of raw steel; rather, they use scrap steel to produce finished products such as pipe, sheet, or construction forms. Mini-mills have grown tremendously since the 1960s (some of the larger are Atlantic, Florida Steel, Georgetown, North Star, and Nucor). About sixty such mills operate today, twice the number operating twenty years ago. Between 1970 and the early 1980s, mini-mill production tripled; in 1981 this new sector of the industry accounted for 15 percent of all domestic shipments (Kirkland 1981b:44). Projections are that as early as 1986, 25 percent of the domestic market will be controlled by mini-mills (*New York Times*: 23 Sept. 1981). According to McManus (1980a:MP5), writing in *Iron Age*:

> The advance of mini-mills is part of a general structural change. The negative part of this change is marked by contraction and stagnation. Less conspicuous but equally important is the positive side. It is worth noting that the growth and expansion of two smaller companies--Nucor Corp. and Florida Steel Corp.--have more than offset the Youngstown shutdowns of United States Steel Corp. and Jones & Laughlin Steel Corp.

While the technology facilitating the development of mini-mills, i.e. electric furnaces, existed since the 1950s, only since the early 1970s has mini-mill growth accelerated. This is due to a combination of factors. Given higher transportation costs resulting from the energy crisis of the 1970s, the smaller mills shipping to local markets have been able to compete successfully with integrated producers shipping to consumers in larger market areas. Also mini-mill corporations have been able to steal specialized product markets away from integrated producers. Unlike integrated producers which are stuck with facilities designed to produce a product mixture geared toward market demand of earlier decades, newly constructed mini-mills are designed to produce items for specialized markets now expanding, e.g. pipe for oil drilling. Not only do mini-mill corporations have the advantage of exclusively producing items for the more profitable markets, but they use newer, more efficient machinery and processes. Also, mini-mill corporations are better able to withstand the costs of economic downturns. According to a prominent economic analyst, the cost of idling a mini-mill for a few months if demand slackens is significantly less than turning off the furnaces at an integrated plant (*New York Times*: 23 Sept. 1983). Thus, all of these factors--product specialization, higher productivity, and relative immunity to the costs of economic downturns--give mini-mills a competitive advantage over integrated producers.

Another major factor helping to keep down mini-mill production costs has been low labor costs due to the relatively low unionization rate in this sector. Non-union labor costs are estimated to be about one-third less than union labor costs in the American steel industry (U.S. Congress 1980:39). There are a number of reasons for the low unionization rate in mini-mills. First, most of the mills are in the South--an area which has traditionally provided a "pro-corporate environment" and has been hostile to unions.[1] Second, the communities where mini-mills are located tend to be smaller and more dependent on the industry (Stenmark). This means that even in those mini-mills that are unionized, the local community is likely to exert pressure on workers to moderate wage demands--particularly if they are perceived as threatening the economic well-being of the mill.[2] Speaking of the South's social and political environment, Roger Regulbrugge, President of Georgetown Steel--one of the mini-mills that is unionized--comments:

> I've noticed a much greater sensitivity on the part of state and local governments to their own interests as they're served by industry. They realize that business' interests are their interests. They're more genuinely concerned about you. It's a good climate in which to do business politically as well as physically [quoted in Barks 1980:28].

Other companies have exploited this environment in resisting unionization. A staff member of the American Iron and Steel Institute remarked that Florida Steel--a company with four mini-mills in the South--has "actively sought" to maintain a "union-free environment" (Stenmark). On the other side of the labor-relations fence, William McGarry--USWA Director of Organizing--calls Florida Steel "our J.P. Stevens." Like the embattled textile producer, Florida Steel has been able to frustrate unionization attempts and contract negotiations by stringing out union and worker appeals in both the National Labor Relations Board system and the Federal courts (McGarry). Despite the fact that the USWA won NLRB union-recognition elections at two Florida Steel plants, they have not been successful in negotiating a contract with the company. Other than at Georgetown Steel in South Carolina, the only other major success by the USWA in organizing mini-mills has been at North Star Steel--one of the few mini-mill companies with plants located in northern states.

In explaining why mini-mills have been so difficult to organize, the USWA's McGarry echoes industry spokespersons, indicating that most mills are in the South with its pro-corporate and anti-union environment. Speaking of organizing experiences in the late 1970s and early 1980s, he notes that "in some communities there has been concerted community action against any [union] organizing. Chambers of Commerce, as well as local and regional industrial development groups have worked against the union" (ibid.). Also, the small workplace size of mini-mills makes them difficult to organize. Given the amount of resources that a union must spend in organizing any workplace, e.g. organizers' salaries, legal fees, and general administration costs, it is much more cost effective to organize larger workplaces, i.e. larger workplaces outside the steel industry. In such larger facilities the "return on investment"--in the form of new members and new dues revenue--is higher. Also, management's ability to nurture close ties and more "paternalistic" supervision policies is greater at smaller workplaces making it more difficult for unions to gain support from a majority of the workers.

Mini-mills are also difficult to organize because they represent decentralized work sites controlled by a centralized corporation. One company may own five or ten plants each employing 500 to 1,000 workers. If the union is to be successful in organizing workers and pressuring the company into signing contracts, a majority of the company's plants need to be organized. However, because the plants are spread around the country, organizing costs are considerable. It is for such reasons that mini-mills have remained largely non-union.

Thus, the bottom line for mini-mills is reduced labor costs. This, combined with the other competitive advantages of the mini-mill corporations discussed earlier, has provided mini-mill corporations with higher profit rates than those achieved by integrated producers. In turn, this has given the small-scale producers a greater ability to attract investment dollars for new development. In 1978, the average return on investment of the top twelve integrated steel companies was 6.2 percent. In contrast, the comparable statistic for the largest fifteen non-integrated companies and specialty steel companies was 11.6 percent (U.S. Congress 1980: Table 14, 122). Mini-mills are growing. According to McManus, writing in *Iron Age*, "Individual corporations have built fairly large networks" of mills rivaling the capacity of many integrated producers (1980a:MP10). Nucor, one such "network," did not build its first mill until 1969 and is now among the top twenty U.S. steel producers (Kirkland 1981:43).

Diversification

The diversification of the industry begun in the 1960s also changed the shape of American steel companies in the 1970s. Throughout the 1970s there was a shift away from investment in basic steel. Four of the largest U.S. producers--U.S. Steel, National Steel, Bethlehem Steel, and Armco--worked to diversify their holdings. By the end of the 1970s, an increased share of revenues in these companies came from production units outside of basic steel. Because non-steel investments have generally provided higher profits for steel companies, the move away from steel investments has been reinforced by the general market.

U.S. Steel--the nation's largest steel producer--led in the shift toward non-steel investments. The company developed oil drilling rig fabrication plants, steel service centers (warehouses that cut and shape steel to order), chemical production facilities, insulation fabrication plants, retailing businesses, and a mortgage company. The revenue for this expansion was obtained through the sale of part of its vast coal reserves, as well as development of other resources it owns, e.g. iron, uranium, oil and gas.

The profitability of non-steel activities has been the stimulus for diversification. For example, before U.S. Steel's takeover of Marathon Oil (discussed in the next chapter), 61 percent of U.S. Steel's assets were in steel and 7 percent were in manufacturing. However, over the five years preceding the takeover, steel provided only 4 percent of its operating income and its oil drilling rig manufacturing division produced a sizeable 33 percent of U.S. Steel's operating income (Kirkland 1981:30, 31). Explaining his company's move away from steel and toward greater diversification, U.S. Steel Chairman David M. Roderick comments, "Let's manage assets we can make money on rather than sit there nursing a sick cow" (ibid.:29). Richard Kirkland, a writer for *Fortune*, observes that U.S. Steel has begun to treat "its non-steel operations as vital businesses in their own right" (ibid.:30).

Other steel companies followed a similar road. Bethlehem's non-steel sales came to 28 percent of its 1980 revenues--an increase from earlier years (McManus 1981:47).

National Steel has successfully moved into the aluminum smelting business as well as financial ventures. Its National Aluminum subsidiary returned over 30 percent on investment--a return unheard of in basic steel (U.S. General Accounting Office 1981:2-26; *Iron Age* 4 May 1981:39). By the end of the 1970s, Armco was further along in diversification than most producers. By 1980, only 53 percent of its assets were invested in the production of carbon steel. As a result of this diversification strategy, Armco has been one of the more profitable "steel" companies (U.S. Congress 1980:122; McManus 1980b).

The combination of more efficient technology and the phase out of old less-efficient facilities contributed to improved basic steel output per manhour through the late 1970s (as shown in Table 4.6). While the American steel industry was still not as efficient as producers in many foreign countries, it was significantly reshaped by the late 1970s. When the American steel industry entered the 1970s, it was still quite dependent on steel production and quite concerned with maintaining labor peace. By the end of the decade, it was much less dependent on steel production, and automation of the steel facilities helped give it more control over the steel labor force that remained. Labor peace was still desirable, but the industry now had more leverage over the workers and over the union. This change influenced both the union and the rank-and-file movement.

THE UNION AND LABOR RELATIONS

The 1970s was also a pivotal decade for the union. Paralleling the steel industry's consolidation of power over the production process, union leaders were consolidating control over their organization. In the early 1970s, the control was not enough to make International union leaders feel absolutely confident in rebuffing a grassroots reform movement. Like the industry, labor peace was important at this crucial stage in power consolidation. Thus, in the first part of this period, the industry and International union negotiated a labor agreement--the Experimental Negotiating Agreement--which provided for substantial increases in real wages along with prohibitions against an industry-wide strike. Although the rank-and-file movement continued to grow in the 1970s, the ENA did take some of the edge off grassroots disenchantment. The industrial peace bought by the ENA gave the industry time to complete its reorganization without disruption. It also gave the International union time in which to further diversify its membership base--reducing the power of the rank-and-file dissidents concentrated in basic steel. By the end of the 1970s, this diversification, combined with the drastic decline in steel employment, had substantially undercut the rank-and-file movement's traditional base of support.

Labor Peace in the Early 1970s

A decade without significant real wage increases had produced rank-and-file unrest. Thus, it was prudent for the industry--which was still reorganizing--and the International union leadership--which was seeing its power gradually increased as a result of membership diversification--to enter into a labor agreement that would both appease an increasingly disenchanted union membership and guard against any major strike that might disrupt industrial production. It was in this context that the industry and the union leadership established the Experimental Negotiating Agreement (ENA).

Adopted in 1972 as a product of private International union:industry talks dating back to the late 1960s, the ENA provided the basic steel membership with significant wage and benefit improvements. Equally important was the ENA provision that the union would not strike at contract expiry and would instead submit to binding arbitration if an agreement had not been reached by a set date.* This gave the industry a guarantee that steady production and profit levels would not be disrupted by the process of customer stockpiling during contract negotiations and the resulting drop in sales after a settlement (Abel 1976:58). Such a no-strike provision is highly unusual in American labor agreements.

Although opposition to the ENA and the forfeiture of the "right to strike" at contract expiry became a major rallying cry of the renewed rank-and-file movement of the 1970s, the wage improvements the ENA brought to basic steelworkers undoubtedly calmed down some disenchanted grassroots union members. Furthermore, the ENA was an ideological tool that could be used to deflect rank-and-file criticism. The ENA was touted as a way of stopping the encroachment of imports onto the American market, and thereby a method for saving American steelworkers' jobs. The argument was that foreign steel producers were likely to get a foothold in the American market during a strike-produced shortage. The growth of imports after the 1959 strike was cited as evidence. However, as already indicated in the discussion of the reorganization of the industry, and as the industry itself demonstrated by its massive plant closings and layoffs of the late 1970s, saving jobs was not a major priority of the industry. Thus, in the years in which it was in effect (1972-80), the ENA functioned as both a political pacifier and a red herring.

---

* Strikes over local issues were allowed under the ENA. However, it was unlikely that large numbers of locals would go out on strike over local issues at any one time. Locals representing one plant of a multi-plant company would not be in a good bargaining position vis-a-vis management when other facilities of that company were still producing steel. Thus, if such local strikes did occur, they were likely to be short ones.

Membership Diversification

During the 1970s, the proportion of basic steel membership in the union was declining. As noted above, this was the result of contraction of the domestic integrated steel industry along with the encroachment into the market by non-union mini-mills and foreign producers. This reduced the size of the constituency which traditionally supported dissident movements in the USWA. Also, because the industrial base of the membership was becoming more diverse, it gave the International more power over the union organization by reducing the influence of the membership in any one industrial sector. Contact between locals of the same industry at union "industrial conferences," bargaining councils, and union conventions has historically been the primary means by which local union members came into contact with each other. Basic steel dissidents have used these official gatherings as opportunities to organize support. However, with membership diversification comes the reduced influence of any one industrial sector regardless of how well it is organized.

While the shift in membership was gradual, it changed the shape of the union by the end of the decade. As shown in Table 5.1, between 1969 and 1980 there was a significant decline in the proportion of primary metal workers--which is composed mainly of basic steel workers. This sector of the union accounted for less than 41 percent of the 1.2 million USWA members in 1980 compared to 52 percent in 1969. The shift was not just caused by changes in industrial employment patterns.

The USWA has followed a conscious policy of membership diversification by merging with smaller unions. While the USWA had merged with one union early in its history--the 45,000 member Aluminum Workers of America in 1944--it engaged in more mergers in recent years. These include mergers with the International Union of Mine-Mill and Smelter Workers in 1967, the 20,000-member United Stone and Allied Products Workers of America in 1971, and the 175,000-member District 50, Allied and Technical Workers in 1972 (United Steelworkers of America 1974). This has contributed to the changes in membership characteristics. It also parallels the trend in union mergers throughout the country (U.S. Department of Labor 1980a:54). Although rank-and-file movement organizations of the 1970s were better organized than earlier movement organizations, their lack of understanding of this metamorphosis in union structure and industry structure hampered their effectiveness. As will be shown in the remainder of this chapter, the 1970s were pivotal years for the rank-and-file movement. The decade saw the strongest rank-and-file challenge to the International leadership in USWA history. It also saw the decline of the movement because of its inability to develop new strategies to deal with changing union and industrial environments.

GROWTH OF RANK-AND-FILE DISSIDENT ORGANIZATIONS

The list of achievements of progressive insurgents in the 1970s includes local union election victories, the growth of districtwide "Right to Strike Committees," a number of district directorship election victories, and a 1977 campaign for International offices that was unsuccessful, but which nevertheless attracted the votes of 250,000 USWA members. Much of the success was fueled by the grassroots unrest already documented. It also was a product of some improvement in organizational strategies compared to previous rank-and-file efforts.

However, despite growing support for reform in the 1970s, new obstacles stood in the way of reform organization growth. Structural and environmental factors beyond the control of movement organizations--most notably union membership diversification and the changing structure of the basic steel industry--hindered development of the insurgency. In addition, the strategies, structures, and political issues adopted by movement organizations themselves stunted the growth of the movement. Most prominent among these stumbling blocks were (1) continued reliance on basic steelworkers for political support instead of development of support in all sectors of the union; (2) lack of a specific program for union organizational reform; (3) reliance on the personality of leaders, rather than on a political program, in making appeals to the membership; and (4) reform organization strategies which led to leadership centralization and discouragement of local grassroots initiative. Just as earlier movement organizations used strategies and issues that did not take into consideration changes in industrial and union organizational environments, so did the rank-and-file movement of the 1970s fail to keep up with changes in union and industry. The movement of the 1970s faced a changing industry and union, using early 1960s strategies. The remainder of this chapter looks first at the nature of *local* caucuses, and second at the development of inter-caucus networks. The next chapter will deal with the growth of a *unionwide* rank-and-file organization in the 1970s.

CHANGES IN THE LOCAL CAUCUSES: THE CASE OF LOCAL 1010

Before closely analyzing the emergence of the unionwide reform movement, it is vital to understand the changing nature of local rank-and-file caucuses at this time. As noted in the previous chapter, the organizational context, as well as the more general social and economic environment, had changed in such a way as to affect caucus structure. Using a survival-of-the-fittest orientation, one can see that only those insurgent organizations capable of withstanding and countering the growing International influence at the local level will survive in a changing environment. Throughout the 1960s--particularly during the late 1960s--the Local 1010 Caucus evolved from a loosely-held-together network led by a few individuals into a more formal organization with a more elaborate leadership structure. Such a tighter "net" was more effective in catching disenchanted shopfloor workers and recruiting them into the rank and file movement. Thus, the growth of local caucuses is a combined function of grassroots disenchantment and more effective organizational nets. Following is an examination of the social process by which the movement expanded at the local level. I will look at (1) what issues and social conditions stimulated initial involvement of rank and filers in the Caucus and (2) how a grassroots leadership emerged which was capable of both organizing workers and articulating demands.

Initial Involvement Stimulated by Individual Grievances

Most activists in the Local 1010 Rank and File Caucus traced their initial involvment in the Caucus to personal grievances they had against the company. Jim Robinson, a young worker at Inland Steel, observed that wages and benefits under the union's contract were not bad, but what disturbed him and many other workers is the lack of control production workers have over workplace decisions. Robinson remarked, "What really irritates people is that...we haven't kept up in terms of rights on the job, working conditions, and safety.... It's what goes on during the eight hours you're in there. This is what constantly aggravates people" (Robinson).

Many activists in the 1970s attributed the beginning of their involvement in union politics to specific workplace "aggravations" or grievances. If the grievance was formally filed and successfully handled by the union, it often represented the beginning of closer contact between the individual and local union officials in a particular department* --usually the griever or steward. In some cases these officials were Rank and File Caucus members who used these official contacts to recruit supporters for the Caucus. In other cases where grievances were not successfully handled by union officials, union members sought out Rank and File Caucus leaders because of their record of criticizing company and union policies. As shown in Table 5.2, more than a third of the 21 rank-and-file activists that I interviewed at Local 1010 identified specific grievances as marking the beginning of their involvement in the union and Caucus. These 21 members of

---

* "Departments" refer to functional units of the steel plant, e.g. a department consisting of 200 workers in a mill producing flat-rolled steel, or a department consisting of 100 workers employed in a maintenance crew that does repair work throughout a large section of the steel-producing complex. Departments may range in size from 100 to 3,000.

the Local 1010 Rank-and-File Caucus represent 70-80 percent of the active Caucus membership, i.e. those who regularly attend Caucus meetings and are involved in caucus activities in between peak activity periods around elections. For example, John Freer, a supporter of the Rank-and-File Caucus since he started work in the early 1950s, first came in contact with Caucus leaders when he filed a grievance because he was denied a promotion for which he had applied. Others identified unfair disciplinary actions. Still others indentified racial, ethnic, or sexual discrimination by the company as the source of the dissatisfaction which brought them into union politics. For example, one Mexican-American mechanic--a 15-year member of the Rank-and-File Caucus--explains that he became involved in union politics because the company discriminated against him. Joe Pena recalls,

> When I first went in I had no choice where I would work. They hired me into the coal processing operation of the coke plant. Most Blacks and Latins were given jobs in the coke ovens, blast furnaces, yard department and open hearth [Pena].

These jobs tended to be dangerous and provided little opportunity for advancement in pay or skill level. A number of Black union activists recalled similar experiences.

Sexual discrimination has also contributed to involvement. Mary Hopper, who became involved in union politics in the 1950s, remembers that when the "boss" would come around, many women "would say their 'Our Fathers' and 'Hail Marys,' hoping that he wouldn't come near them. They were afraid of them. It was fear. You couldn't stand up for your rights." However, continues Hopper, "a few brave souls, a little at a time" would not take the abuse any more. "There's always a breaking point when you figure, 'The heck with [it], I'm going to fight this'" (Hopper). Hopper first became involved when a friend introduced her to a union activist who convinced them that some of their problems could be solved by the union if they joined together. Another young Caucus member recalls how Jim Balanoff, the leader of the Local 1010 Rank and File Caucus, "recruited" him into the Caucus and into union politics:

> Jim actively sought young people to get involved in the Caucus. Balanoff was the force that got me involved. He won't give up, he'll latch on to a guy and talk until a guy finally comes to the Caucus meeting. He's a fantastic worker, the Caucus would fall apart without him [Olszanski].

Six of the thirteen respondents who cited personal contact were brought into the Caucus by Balanoff. This leads to the question, "How do leaders emerge in the workplace?"

Emergence of Leadership and Personal Contact

In the case of Jim Balanoff and many other leaders of the Caucus, their jobs in the mill required them to move around the steel plant; this facilitated contact with other workers. For a long time, Balanoff worked on a crane repair gang that moved around to many different mills and shops throughout the plant. This provided him with the opportunity to contact a large number of workers. In addition to job mobility, employment in a large department can contribute to leadership roles. A number of Caucus members who work in large departments, e.g. the mill which fabricates 80-inch wide sheets of steel and employs 3,000, have also emerged as leaders because of their contact with relatively large numbers of workers.

The style of personal interaction is also significant in recruitment. In the 1970s, Local 1010 Rank and File Caucus leaders emphasized the need to establish on-the-job social ties with as many fellow workers as possible. Balanoff, who once lost a local election by fewer than 100 votes out of 3,000 cast, recalled a post-election conversation with a fellow worker, who told Balanoff that he did not vote for him because when Balanoff passed by him every morning in the mill on his way to work, he never once said, "Hello." Through personal contact the Caucus organization gained visibility. Hence, it emphasized development of networks in each department so that workers come in contact with Caucus members on a daily basis. Jim Robinson observed that the most effective political organizing occurs from the bottom up rather than from the top down; that is, the forging of social and political ties in each department has more impact than general plantwide politicking by the Caucus (Robinson).

This also applies to Caucus organizing off the job. Social networks established in the community by Caucus activists are also important to their strength in the union. It is no coincidence that when compared to the geographical distribution of all steelworkers, a larger proportion of Caucus leaders live in communities close to the mill. An individual activist's proximity to the mill is positively related to his prominence as a rank-and-file leader. There are two reasons for this. First, such an individual is closer to millgate taverns, clubs, and other meeting places that facilitate contact with various social networks of workers. Since these social networks are the primary spheres of recruitment into the reform movement, an individual activist who is involved in such a social setting will have greater opportunity to build a personal contact network and emerge as a leader. One activist in the Local 1010 Rank and File Caucus who lives in Indiana Harbor--the community adjacent to the steel mill--observed that many workers living 20 or 30 miles from the plant just try to beat the rush hour after work and do not frequently stop at the local bars or coffee shops like many of those who live nearby (Mills). This also means that Blacks, Hispanics and older white workers--those groups that populate the community close to the mills--are disproportionately more involved in union and rank-and-file politics than are other workers.

A second reason for the greater leadership role and general involvement among workers who live close to the mill is the nature of the neighborhoods themselves. Workers living in homogeneous blue-collar neighborhoods such as those in East Chicago, Gary, and Chicago's Eastside, are more likely to find the community supportive of militant union activity. These neighborhoods have long had a strong identification with the workplace and the union. With the possible exception of steelworker wives and daughters who work as secretaries in downtown Chicago, most persons living in these neighborhoods rarely venture outside the community (Kornblum 1974:ch 1).[3] It is in these millgate neighborhoods that generations of families have been packing lunch pails early every morning on their way to the mills. Older residents of these communities can tell their sons and daughters of the battles to organize steelworkers in the 1930s--battles such as the Memorial Day Massacre which left ten steelworker pickets dead at the hands of the Chicago police. This tradition creates a "community consciousness" as a young South Chicago steelworker explains:

> There's a certain consciousness, an anti-company consciousness. They live in the same area. People here see their children and their fathers working in the steel mill--that might be one reason for [the militancy in some of the Chicago area locals] [R. Wood].

The role of workers' families in shaping their interest in union politics is also apparent. Many rank-and-file activists recall their fathers' own union involvement as well as the parental encouragement they received regarding involvement in union politics. Some remember their parents discussing how active unionists weathered the frustrating days of the 1950s McCarthy era, while fathers of others recounted the great strikes of 1919.[4] A typical account was that of a father who nurtured a positive image of unions by his own involvement in union politics,

> He came from the old country in 1918 and spoke broken English, but he went to every union meeting he could.... He never had any ambition to run for union office. He felt that it was his responsibility to go to meetings to vote, to be a part, to see that his union was run properly. They used to give out union buttons each year or two. He had these buttons all over his cap and was proud of it [Olszanski].

The thread that ran through the backgrounds of many rank-and-file leaders in the 1970s was not so much parental involvement in progressive union politics as it was parental involvement in the union. With this understanding of the individual motivations for joining local reform caucuses, we now turn to a discussion of how the movement expanded beyond the local level.

SPREAD OF THE MOVEMENT BEYOND ONE LOCAL

The spread of the rank-and-file reform movement has two dimensions. The first dimension is the spread to other locals, i.e. the formation of additional, relatively autonomous local reform organizations. Second is the spread to higher organizational levels, e.g. to districtwide, industrywide, or unionwide levels. Although the case study presented here documents the growth of an *indigenous* rank-and-file caucus, rank-and-file activity has picked up in some locals because of contact and support from rank-and-file activists *outside* the local. Indigenous social networks alone have not always provided the momentum necessary to form a local rank-and-file reform organization. Rather, rank-and-filers from locals with indigenous networks (which I will call first-generation caucuses) have initiated districtwide organizations which subsequently have facilitated the development of rank-and-file networks in other locals lacking well-developed indigenous networks (these new caucuses I will call second-generation caucuses). However, once given outside support, these second-generation caucuses grow because the working conditions, grievances, and workplace social structures are similar to those in the workplaces which have produced first-generation caucuses. Thus, they become self-sufficient after the initial boost from first-generation caucuses.

The Local 1010 Rank and File Caucus and two or three other first-generation caucuses were instrumental in organizing the District 31 Right to Strike Committee in 1973, formed to oppose the ENA. They also provided the core for Ed Sadlowski's District Directorship races of 1973-74, and his International Presidency race in 1977 (discussed in the next chapter). Prior to the formation of these regional groups, organized rank-and-file activity was not apparent in some large locals in District 31. However, contact with the Right to Strike Committee organizers--who collected 10,000 signatures in Chicago locals--and work with the Sadlowski District 31 Directorship campaigners--who ultimately got their candidate elected--provided the rallying point for the few union dissidents there were in area local unions. The previously isolated militants saw the new groups as viable vehicles for affecting political change in locals with unresponsive leaders or administrations marked by corruption.

For example, an organized rank-and-file caucus did not exist at Youngstown Sheet and Tube in East Chicago (Local 1011) prior to 1973 even though the plant is adjacent to Inland Steel's plant. Norm Purdue, elected president of Local 1011 in

1976, recalled the beginnings of the Youngstown Sheet and Tube plant caucus: "It started in the bottom of a tavern, Little John's Tavern. There were eight or ten people then. But it grew to the point that we...[were successful] in the Sadlowski election. We knew we could do it again" (Purdue).

However, one cannot assume that the spread of the reform movement to other locals within a District is equivalent to the spread to higher organizational levels. In the 1970s, many of the local caucuses remained autonomous and resisted or did not actively support districtwide organizations. Other than at the height of election campaigns, many local activists were unaware of the political activities of other caucuses in nearby plants. In the 1979 local union elections, a number of reform caucus leaders who were elected in the 1976 reform surge (particularly in District 31) lost their offices; one factor contributing to these losses was the lack of support from other caucuses.

The districtwide and unionwide organizations that have existed in District 31 have been passing phenomena rather than permanent organizations. The 1973 Right to Strike group and the 1973-74 Sadlowski District Directorship campaign organization, as well as the 1977 Steelworkers Fight Back organization, were transient organizations that did not develop permanent constituencies. These regional and national groups had only *indirect* links to shopfloor workers. Many of the more prominent local rank-and-file leaders supporting the campaigns brought with them their collection of personal contacts that they had collected over the years. In many respects these larger organizations were passing alliances between autonomous local rank-and-file reform organizations.

Regional and national organizations did not have the characteristics of local organizations. Rather, they had a qualitatively different organizational character. They were not based on personal contact with shopfloor workers. Rather, they were based on broad political campaigns which made impersonal appeals to rank-and-filers. As the political focus moved from local to districtwide to unionwide levels, *personal* networks became less significant and the reform movement's *organizational* structure became more significant. The problem this caused for the unionwide spread of the rank-and-file movement is the subject of the next chapter.

Chapter 6

Sadlowski and the Rise of Steelworkers Fight Back 1976–1979

Steelworkers Fight Back was the most prominent rank-and-file movement organization in the USWA during the 1970s. It was also the best organized unionwide challenge to the International leadership in the union's history. Fight Back was the organization behind the 1977 electoral challenge to USWA International leaders. The present analysis has implications not only for future rank-and-file organizations in the USWA, but also for rank-and-file organizations in other union organizations--particularly for rank-and-file organizations that are in industrial unions and in industries that have experienced structural changes which have paralleled those in the USWA and the steel industry.

THE CHANGING POLITICAL ENVIRONMENT

While Pittsburgh and Youngstown had been the home bases of previous insurgent organizations, the Chicago-Northwest Indiana USWA District (USWA District 31) was the focus of the 1970s insurgency. There were two major reasons for this. First, in the 1960s and early 1970s, District 31 basic steel membership grew because of steel industry expansion in the Midwest. With the opening of Bethlehem Steel's new Burns Harbor, Indiana plant and continued expansion of other mills in the area--particularly Inland Steel in East Chicago, Indiana--District 31 represented the largest concentration of basic steelworkers in any USWA district. Second, the District 31 Director of thirty-one years was retiring. This provided an opportunity for a challenger to run against a non-incumbent--a situation which increased the chances of success for the grassroots challenger.

There were also more general factors--not specific to District 31--contributing to the rise in organized unionwide rank-and-file activity in the early 1970s. Anti-International candidates had won key local union presidencies throughout the union in 1970. Although they still represented a minority of District 31 presidents, the small number of newly elected reformers did lend greater credibility to rank-and-file criticism of the International. USWA activists were also encouraged by the political mood outside the union, especially by the December 1972 victory of the Miners for Democracy (MFD) in ousting a corrupt administration in the coal miners' union. MFD had obtained help, not only from liberal lawyers and political activists, but from the Federal government itself, which had intervened to overturn a fraudulent election. This was especially reassuring to USWA dissidents in 1973, since past USWA challengers had suspected that election fraud in their union had contributed to past failures (G. Patterson). Beyond the immediate union environment there was also a general mood of dissidence. The anti-war movement continued to swell in the early 1970s and by this period the movement for racial equality of the 1960s had made an impact on industrial communities and unions.

THE RISE OF ED SADLOWSKI

It was in this political setting that Edward Sadlowski, as a local union president from the East Side of Chicago, emerged as candidate for District 31 Director and later for International President. Sadlowski set himself apart from other union leaders by painting himself as a "maverick." In the District 31 Directorship campaign, Sadlowski called for a few specific union reforms, e.g. membership ratification of dues increases and contracts. However, he relied more on his reputation and general political statements to differentiate himself from incumbent union officials. On union democracy he stated, "We either continue to give one or two men the power to affect our lives, or we can create a union that gives all of its members an equal voice in decision making" (Sadlowski for District 31 Director 1973a, 1973b, 1974).   On political and social issues outside the union, he took a strong stand against the Vietnam War (United Steelworkers of America 1968:223).   He spoke of the "working class" and "class action."* Some Steelworkers dismissed Sadlowski's militant talk as "rhetoric" and "political maneuvering."   However, the fact remains that the maverick image that Sadlowski built for himself served as a springboard in his electoral quests.

Ed Sadlowski's District 31 campaign in 1973 was organized by himself, along with a handful of friends and fellow Steelworkers.   In February 1972, Sadlowski and ten other persons gathered in a South Chicago bar to discuss a strategy and program for organizing a reform campaign.   By the end of the year, this campaign organization had grown to include other local unionists, but Sadlowski and his close supporters still directed much of the campaign.   Despite attempts by International staff representatives to frustrate Sadlowski's campaigners, this group succeeded in convincing the majority of local union members at forty local unions to endorse Sadlowski, giving him enough local union nominations to place him on the 1973 ballot (Askins; Conroy 1977:112).**

However, Sadlowski lost the 1973 District election to the candidate backed by the International leadership and outgoing District Director.   The margin was slim--less than 1,800 votes out of 45,000 cast.   Ironically, it was this loss and the outside attention and support that it attracted that caused the insurgency in the Midwest District to bloom.   Charges of vote fraud attracted lawyers who had previously guided court battles for the Miners for Democracy.   Investigators from the U.S. Department of Labor became involved in the dispute, vote

---

* Speaking about the problems facing urban blacks, Sadlowski stated: "I'm a strong advocate of class action.   I'm a strong advocate of taking to the streets if necessary.   In many respects, sometimes the ballot box doesn't really reflect the pent-up emotion of people" (*Washington Post* 1975).

** Sadlowski's opponent, Samuel Evett, collected more than 240 nominations.   The International staff--the vast majority of which supported Evett--used various tactics to frustrate Sadlowski's supporters from attending local union nominating meetings, e.g. by holding meetings at different times or days than previously scheduled so that only the staff and local union members friendly to Evett would be informed to attend. One staff representative recalls a meeting of District 31 staffpersons at which Joseph Germano, the retiring director, "encouraged" representatives to donate money to Evett.   A formal motion passed at this meeting required all staffpersons to donate $200 to Evett's campaign (Graczyk).

fraud was documented, the first election was nullified, and a new election was scheduled.

With the help of this outside support and exploitation of the fraud issue--which had been widely reported in both the regional and national media--Sadlowski won the rerun by a 2:1 margin. The election was marked with an unusually high voter turnout.* The effectiveness of the corruption issue was, in part, attributable to the backdrop of the Watergate scandal and President Nixon's August 1974 resignation, which made most Americans take a closer look at the integrity of all elected officials. Also, the outside help and media coverage had increased both the size of Sadlowski's campaign organization and its ability to get its message to the membership. However, despite this victory, the new District Director had little opportunity to affect International union decision making.

Given the structure of the USWA, a District Director does not hold much power. Even though a Director's vote on the International Executive Board--the USWA's major policy-making body outside of the convention--is determined by the size of the district represented by the Director, a Director from even the largest District only has a small fraction of the IEB vote. Moreover, all staffpersons working in a District are appointed by the International leadership. Therefore the significance of the District 31 victory was not one of political power.

NEW LEGITIMACY FOR THE RANK-AND-FILE MOVEMENT

The 1974 insurgent victory, however, did increase the political legitimacy of the rank-and-file movement. Because this legitimacy facilitated mobilization of political resources, e.g. contributions of money and labor to insurgent organizations, it had the potential of leading to the acquisition of more power. "Legitimacy" refers here to the acceptance by potential supporters of a movement's political ideology and program as a realistic alternative to existing organizational ideology and program. Sociologists have stressed that legitimacy plays an important role in helping organizations and their leaders maintain control over resources. In *Organizational Design*, Jeffrey Pfeffer states that legitimacy "ensures continued social

---

* One example of the Sadlowski organization's use of the fraud issue is a 1974 campaign handbill in tabloid newspaper format which contained a series of short articles with headlines such as "District Leader's [Evett's] Credibility at a Low Ebb," "Moral Downfall of a Labor Leader," "The Chronology of a Stolen Election," and "Corrupt Elective Process Deprives Members of Choice." In addition, more than fifty articles and editorials from local and national newspapers discussing the 1973 vote fraud case were reproduced and distributed by Sadlowski campaigners (Askins; Sadlowski for District Director 1974).

approval and the ability of the organization to claim the resources required to continue its activities" (1978:159). Similarly, legitimacy must be seen as an important resource to social movements attempting to challenge the power of existing organizations or incumbent office holders.

Within the union, this legitimacy meant that rank-and-file union members were more likely to respond positively to pleas for support from Sadlowski and the broader reform movement. Instead of being viewed as "crackpots" or "left-wing extremists," they now appeared more down-to-earth and realistic. Cliff ("Cowboy") Mezo, a Local 1010 Rank and File Caucus member who was elected as Local Union Trustee in 1976, remarks that Sadlowski's victory, combined with his endorsement of local union anti-International activity, "gave us legitimacy, status" (Mezo). Because of this, in 1976 local union elections, rather than viewing challengers as dark horses who deserved little attention, union members took the insurgents more seriously. Local 65 activist Joe Kransdorf explains that the 1974 Directorship victory "created a bridge" between those who were always active in progressive rank-and-file politics and those who had been less committed, but nevertheless sympathetic to reform (Kransdorf). Increased legitimacy transformed these latent rank-and-file activists--those who were sympathetic but never felt their involvement would make any difference--into into active supporters.

Outside the union, legitimacy meant that the media was even more likely to treat Sadlowski and fellow insurgents "seriously," thus providing an invaluable means for insurgent leaders and organizations--blocked from use of internal union communication media--to rally support. As Harvey Molotch points out in his article, "Media and Movements":

> Social movements represent those portions of society that lie outside the ordinary routines of exercising power and influence. For them, the mass media represent a potential mechanism for utilizing an establishment institution to fulfill nonestablishemnt goals: communicating with movement followers, reaching out to potential recruits, neutralizing would-be opponents, and confusing or otherwise immobilizing committed opponents [1979:71].

The newly gained legitimacy, media coverage, and support from pockets of supporters in some of the District's large locals helped the rank-and-file movement to grow in the Chicago area. According to Jim Robinson, a Northwest Indiana Steelworker, a "kind of loose" districtwide organization evolved out of Sadlowski's Directorship races. He observes: "A lot of people from here, there and everywhere didn't know each other until they started coming in around Sadlowski" (Robinson). Media coverage and contacts with rank-and-filers from neighboring locals bolstered the confidence of previously isolated dissidents--particularly those in smaller locals. It helped them to overcome problems in formulating their own local rank-and-file caucus programs and strategies. Explains Joe Pena, an activist in Gary, Indiana, "you get an idea of what kind of problems these guys [in other local caucuses] are having ... and what kind of solutions they've found and vice versa" (Pena).

The organizational growth resulting from the improved legitimacy and communication was demonstrated by success in the 1976 local union elections. Prior to these elections fewer than 30 percent of District 31's members were in locals led by supporters of the reform movement. After the election supporters controlled locals representing more than 80 percent of the District membership (C. Balanoff). This turnaround included some decisive defeats of local union candidates openly backed by International leaders. (An example of the open backing was the cooperation of International officials in appearing with incumbents, who were facing strong electoral challenges, at dinners and other special events. It does not seem to be coincidental that these events were scheduled just before the elections and were widely reported in area newspapers [(Hammond, Indiana) Compass, 1976)].) Insurgent candidates won by 2:1 margins at two of the USWA's largest locals--18,000-member Local 1010 at Inland Steel in East Chicago, Indiana, and 9,000-member Local 65 at U.S. Steel's South Works in Chicago. In both these locals reform slates won nearly all the top offices.

Elsewhere in Northwest Indiana, pro-Sadlowski challengers won at Youngstown Sheet and Tube, U.S. Steel's Sheet and Tube Mill, National Steel's Midwest Mill and Bethlehem's Burns Harbor complex. On the Chicago side of the District, insurgent victories were recorded from the smaller foundries on the South Side to can-manufacturing locals on the West Side. Although the major gains were in basic steel locals, one large 3,000-member utility workers' local in northern Indiana put Sadlowski supporters into office. In these local union elections, which are held simultaneously throughout the USWA's more than 5,000 locals, District 31 victories represented the most noticeable shift toward anti-International forces. However, there were anti-International candidates elected in a number of locals outside the Chicago district--the most prominent gains were in basic steel locals in Cleveland and Youngstown, Ohio; Aliquippa, Pennsylvania; Buffalo, New York; and Fontana, California (Nyden 1976).

CHANGING FOCUS FROM REGIONAL TO UNIONWIDE LEVELS

Given the centralization of decision making in the union, it was logical for leaders of the rank-and-file movement to raise their political sights to the International level. Most of the reforms proposed by Sadlowski and other District 31 insurgents could only be changed by International union decision-making bodies. Such reforms included (1) membership right to vote on all dues increases, contracts, and agreements; (2) improvement of pension and hospitalization plans; (3) opposition to job combinations and speedups; (4) implementation of separate industry conferences at the District level instead of just at the International level; (5) improvement of wages; and (6) improvement of training for local grievancemen and International staff representatives (Steelworkers Fight Back 1976, 1977).

While it was obvious that the movement had to move to the International level because that is where decisions were made, it was less obvious that grassroots activists would be able to successfully move from regional organizing to unionwide organizing. The movement, headstrong because of successes in one district, was making a leap--from political activity in a district representing 130,000 union members in a few hundred locals, contained within a relatively small geographical area, to political activity in an International union representing 1.2 million members in over 5,000 locals in the United States, Canada, and Puerto Rico.

STEELWORKERS FIGHT BACK

In 1975, Steelworkers Fight Back--an organization with the stated intention of building a lasting unionwide rank-and-file network--was formed by backers of the Sadlowski USWA International Presidency candidacy. Fight Back leaders stated that Fight Back was not merely a Sadlowski campaign organization; they stated that it was an organization aimed at developing local and regional rank-and-file networks that could ultimately place political pressure on International union leaders--whether they be "reformers" or supporters of present USWA policies (C. Balanoff). Despite these stated intentions, Fight Back became a campaign organization that grew with Sadlowski's candidacy and disappeared with his eventual electoral defeat. This section of the chapter analyzes both the degree to which Steelworkers Fight Back failed to transcend the shortcomings of previous movement organizations, and the extent to which changes in the union and industry undermined efforts of movement organizations in the 1970s.

Central Leadership

Early development of Steelworkers Fight Back was centrally controlled by ten to fifteen individuals who had been supportive of Sadlowski in earlier campaigns. This leadership was unlike the centralized leadership of more established organizations, which controls a more permanent, formal organizational structure through well-defined organizational rules. The Fight Back leadership was a small social network that was trying to *build* such an organization around themselves. Structures and processes were not always formalized, the small network set the policies and procedures. They were not accountable to a recognizable membership. No formal organizational structure or internal election mechanisms were used to build Fight Back's leadership core. Even after the campaign was launched, Fight Back continued to function without formal leadership or structure. Its early organizers described Fight Back as "issue-oriented" and did not develop any organizational structure designed to ensure a voice for rank-and-file Steelworkers (C. Balanoff).

The persons in positions of authority were close friends of Sadlowski both inside and outside of the USWA.[1] Among the more prominent leaders was Clem Balanoff. A steelworker in Youngstown Sheet and Tube's East Chicago plant for seventeen years before retiring, Balanoff ran a small income tax counseling service on Chicago's Southeast Side in 1977. Balanoff had been one of Sadlowski's initial backers in 1972 and remained a key supporter. More than any other one individual, the former steelworker ran the day-to-day affairs of Fight Back--work assignments, leafleting, scheduling rallies and answering inquiries from supporters.

Aside from Clem Balanoff, other close Sadlowski backers included Jim Balanoff, Clem's brother and the Local 1010 President who was later elected to the District 31 Directorship in 1977. Jim Balanoff and at least four other past or present USWA local union officers served as strategists and advisors to Sadlowski and Fight Back, not as administrators of routine activities. A few individuals outside the USWA were influential in Fight Back's decision-making. Sadlowski's brother-in-law as well as at least one prominent official in another International union were influential in the organization. Joseph Rauh, a labor lawyer who had represented UMW candidate Joseph Yablonski and the Miners for Democracy, also had an impact on Fight Back policy--particularly in drafting campaign strategies relying on legal resources.

Day-to-Day Leadership

In addition to the more influential leaders of Fight Back were campaign advisors who affected Fight Back policies and actions by virtue of their positions as administrators of day-to-day campaign affairs. Among these people was George Terrell, who had been active throughout the early 1976 organizing efforts.   Another campaign administrator, Ed James, was hired by Fight Back in the summer of 1976 because of his past involvement in the successful MFD challenge in the United Mine Workers of America.   James provided leadership not only in daily affairs, such as in overseeing content and distribution of campaign leaflets, but also played a role in setting strategy and policy.   James, however, left before the February 1977 election because he was disenchanted with restrictions on his role in determining campaign policy.

These two workers in the central office (consisting of about twenty regular paid and volunteer workers) exerted considerable influence over the campaign because of their control over day-to-day affairs.   Similarly, the approximately thirty to forty individuals appointed and paid by Fight Back to conduct the campaign in districts outside of Chicago influenced policy by controlling information.   (Funds to pay these individuals and to finance other campaign activities were raised by soliciting donations, from persons both inside and outside the union, and by running raffles, dinners, and bazaars.) Many of these individuals were close political friends of Sadlowski from District 31 who were dispatched to run the campaign in the distant regions.

As for formal membership, Fight Back had none. Steelworkers were enlisted as supporters for Fight Back, but other than being listed in a file of names and addresses, they had no formal role in the organization.   By November 1976, Fight Back had accumulated a list of over 1,000 supporters or "contacts" throughout the United States and Canada.   Most of the list consisted of USWA members who had sent in coupons clipped from a leaflet distributed at large plants around the country in the summer of 1976.   The 1976 leafleting campaign was part of Fight Back's union-wide effort initiated in 1975. The purposes of early campaign strategies were to (1) give Sadlowski and Steelworkers Fight Back exposure throughout the union and (2) build the list of "contacts," described above, which would serve as an army of campaigners in the 1977 International election.

Centralized Leadership and Resource Mobilization

The leadership of Fight Back faced a dilemma familiar to leaders of many other movement organizations.   On the one hand, leaders wanted to maintain control over their organization.   On the other hand, without giving supporters some role in the organization, it was difficult to recruit backers and keep them committed to the organization.   Because Fight Back leaders wanted to maintain central control over the organization, they found it increasingly difficult to get supporters to contribute personal time and resources to the campaign without receiving some rewards for their support, e.g. involvement in decision making.   One perspective in social movement literature stresses this utilitarian aspect of social movement organization recruitment of members.

The resource-mobilization view contends that mobilization of individuals in support of a movement or movement organization will occur only if the value of selective incentives is high relative to the individual's costs of involvement (Olson 1968; Fireman & Gamson 1979). Political incentives for an individual rank-and-file union member to actively campaign for an insurgent candidate include (1) potential long-run indirect benefits that he and other union members might receive as a result of reforms made by the candidate if he is elected, (2) long-run personal benefits if the candidate wins office and appoints him to some union position, (3) short-run personal benefits if the supporter becomes better known in his workplace or local union and therefore increases his visibility and political strength in the local setting, and (4) short-run personal benefits due to the increase in personal political power as a result of having direct input into the insurgent campaign and indirect input into union politics. As they are listed here, the first incentive is the weakest and the fourth is the strongest. One of Fight Back's major strategic blunders was to rely on the first, rather diffuse, incentive in mobilizing support. This preserved central control, but limited recruitment. Very late in the campaign Fight Back leaders realized the drawback of this strategy, but were unable to reverse the negative impact in the few months remaining in the campaign.

It should be pointed out here that this utilitarian logic is not the only way of understanding the growth of social movements. Agreement with a movement's ideology is also a reason why individuals support a particular movement. Fight Back relied heavily on this early in the campaign. However, while ideology may attract supporters, the utilitarian incentives are more effective in getting supporters to contribute major amounts of personal resources, e.g. time, money, and political reputation, to the movement. This is particularly the case when movement is functioning within an organizational environment, i.e. the union, which already has values and norms leading members to expect that political activity should lead to personal rewards, such as mobility within the union hierarchy.

Lack of Rank-and-File Input

Nevertheless, early in the electoral campaign, Fight Back was reticent to allow supporters, particularly those outside Chicago, to take an active role in determining campaign strategies and issues. Fight Back attempted to run everything from Chicago. Initially, the formation of local organizations was discouraged; individual supporters received instructions directly from Chicago or from Chicago organization-appointed campaign leaders. Areas that Fight Back leaders had identified as potential sources of strong electoral support--because of the political climate or the large concentration of union members--were controlled more closely by the central leadership.* These districts included Pittsburgh, Cleveland, Detroit, Baltimore, Los Angeles, Buffalo, Birmingham, Hamilton (Ontario, Canada), and Sudbury (Ontario, Canada). In many of these areas, Sadlowski supporters from Chicago were sent to manage campaigns. One observer noted that

> the Sadlowski people in Chicago have been reluctant to let rank and filers elsewhere take initiative. There has been a desire that no literature be used in the campaign except literature prepared at the Chicago headquarters [Rusticus 1977:76].**

Also, communications between Steelworkers Fight Back's central headquarters and supporters outside Chicago were often poor. John DelVecchio, a supporter in the Northeast, commented that many rank-and-file supporters outside the Chicago area expected to receive notification of Fight Back's policy statements and campaign activities. He suggested that the organization might have distributed a union-wide newsletter. Instead, DelVecchio notes that significant campaign developments were not systematically reported to supporters. DelVecchio received most of his information from the media, particularly the left press such as the *Militant* and the *Daily World* (DelVecchio).

In the Chicago District itself, communication to Fight Back supporters was limited and policy input was low; central Fight Back leaders made most policy decisions. "Rank-and-file" meetings were held in Chicago, but according to one activist, the gatherings only discussed problems people were having "getting the message across," the content of leaflets, upcoming rallies, raffle ticket sales, and plant-gate

---

* This was noted by a number of rank-and-file activists whom I interviewed: J. Balanoff, Berlin, Danzey, Dowling, Julian, Kransdorf, B. Morris, and Riehle.

Another factor which many Pittsburgh rank and filers point to is the centralization of what little Pittsburgh organization existed. A staffperson from the International office, Pat Coyne, led the campaign there. Only limited rank-and-file input was invited. Pittsburgh decision-making flowed through Chicago, often delaying important campaign decisions (Anonymous; McMills; Piccirilli).

** On the other hand, in areas where Fight Back leaders did not expect much support, such as in St. Louis and Houston, they allowed local rank-and-file activists to run the campaign with little interference. This absence of central Fight Back control over these areas was also, in part, the result of a shortage of campaign staff. Limited manpower required Fight Back to set priorities and dispatch paid staff to the more promising areas.

leafleting. Policy statements to be made by Sadlowski generally were not discussed (Anonymous--Chicago; Anonymous--Hammond). A Chicago supporter criticized the organization because "not enough Steelworkers were drawn into the campaign to play a leadership role. It was a top-down thing" (Anonymous--Chicago).

ROLE OF THE MEDIA

While the movement's premature leap from district to unionwide activity may have been attributable, in part, to the excitement that any movement experiences after major gains in strength, it was also an accommodating reaction to media attention already given to the movement. Without this media attention the movement would have had to rely more heavily on grassroots communications networks, and hence on the development of localized grassroots support. However, with such attention, particularly national attention, the movement was able to move from local to national activity without developing strong grassroots support networks. In a sense, the media was molding the structure of the rank-and-file movement in the USWA.

National coverage of Sadlowski--a colorful, outspoken union leader in a field of less flamboyant American labor leaders--had catapulted the steelworker into the national limelight. Before Sadlowski announced his candidacy for International President in 1977 USWA elections, Mike Wallace of CBS TV's widely watched *60 Minutes* visited South Chicago and Indiana Harbor to interview Sadlowski and film some of the April 1976 campaigning for local union elections. Before and after Sadlowski announced his candidacy, writers from publications as diverse as the *Wall Street Journal* and *Penthouse* wooed Sadlowski to get interviews.[2] National newspaper headlines read, "Maverick Fighting to Be President of Steelworkers," "Oil-Can Eddie Taking on the Old Guard," and "A Young Turk Frightens the Old Bulls of Big Labor" (Kotz 1976; *Los Angeles Times* 1976; *Village Voice* 1975). Sadlowski was described variously as a "dissident" and "insurgent," "a down-to-earth guy who...never forgets where he came from" (*New York Times* 1976; *Newsweek* 1976; *Youngstown Vindicator* 1976). After the election, *Wall Street Journal* reporter David Ignatius reflected on the role of the media in the campaign. He argued that the press "lovingly dispensed" Sadlowski's maverick "puffery," making him "a momentary liberal cult figure" (Ignatius 1977:26).

In addition to prematurely pushing the rank-and-file movement from a regional success to national stature, the media also influenced the movement's own self perception and structure. It emphasized Sadlowski as an individual, rather than as a leader of a larger, more complex grassroots movement. Sadlowski's personality and personal political style were stressed, rather than the nature of the rank-and-file movement. Accommodation of the rank-and-file movement to this image painted by newspaper, magazine, radio, and television reporters and commentators became a key weakness of the movement. Rather than emphasize grassroots organization as the primary political strategy, a significant amount of time and resources were spent in attracting media attention. Paralleling Fight Back's decision to use strategies aimed at stimulating media attention rather than grassroots organization was its decision to rely on the court system as a key source of political power.

LEGAL RESOURCES AS SOURCES OF POWER

An emphasis on legal maneuvering in lieu of stronger grassroots organizing efforts weakened the movement in the long run. It did provide Fight Back with some important information and political rights, such as access to addresses of USWA locals, restriction on incumbents' use of union publications for electioneering during the immediate campaign period, and preservation of local union nomination votes that the International leadership attempted to disqualify because of technicalities. However, it distracted the organization from building grassroots support.

As with the role of the media in molding campaign strategies and movement organizational structure, the emphasis on a legal campaign was a product of the broader political and social environment in which the movement was operating. Use of court decisions and Federal agency rulings is a relatively effective method of countering the power of a centralized incumbent union leadership. Results of such a strategy are more immediate and have more of a unionwide impact than do strategies involving grassroots organizing. In effect it is a way of increasing the movement's political power by "annexing" the power of the courts or Federal agency to the movement's existing political resources.

However, there is a contradiction here. A legal strategy does appear to be an efficient use of a movement organization's resources at early stages; but in the long run it leads to instability because it creates the illusion of strength at national levels and perpetuates the underdevelopment of broad based grassroots support. The movement is dependent on this outside power source; however, the source is not a dependable and easily-controlled source. Other courts at other times may overrule existing decisions and Federal agencies may reverse policies. If the legal-system source of power disappears, the movement organization that is left is a mere organizational skeleton, lacking substantial support from union members.

IMPACT OF UNION STRUCTURE ON STEELWORKERS FIGHTBACK

The organizational setting in which the campaign took place also influenced the development of the rank-and-file movement. The union's official structures and information networks were largely inaccessible to Fight Back. Clearly, the insurgent organization had no control over what was put into *Steel Labor*, the union newspaper. (Although a court order prohibited the publication of any obvious campaign material supporting the incumbent's choice in the period immediately prior to the election, "indirect" comments and the past published record of International union leadership criticism of rank-and-file dissident activity certainly did not help the reformers.) Nor did the insurgent organization have access to the union's communication network, which ranged from formal and informal contact with hundreds of staff representatives to planning speaking engagements for the International leadership's candidates at official union functions. However, in trying to fight the International at its own game, Fight Back relied heavily on the few staffpersons it did have on its side. This paralleled Fight Back's use of the media and the legal system, in that the insurgent organization was using as much of the legitimate organizational authority, i.e. friendly staffpersons, as it could. In many areas, contact with friendly staff representatives was used in lieu of building local grassroots support. This led to tensions between rank-and-filers and staff representatives in Fight Back.

Fight Back's use of staffpersons was a product of the organizational environment. First, as one rank-and-filer observed, Sadlowski "felt more comfortable with the staff because that's who he saw, that's where he operated. He was a staffman" (Mann). Second, because Fight Back was trying to organize a campaign in a relatively short period of time, it did not have the time to test and evaluate which local rank-and-file groups had broad-based support and which ones were paper organizations. Therefore, Fight Back went where it "felt the built-in support was--a few staffmen here and there" (Mann). Staffpersons have contacts at both large and small locals by virtue of their jobs; this was helpful in building a wide array of campaign contacts.

Third, staffpersons generally were political moderates; their support provided the Sadlowski camp with ammunition with which to counter red-baiting. This was most apparent in Sadlowski's choice of staff representatives as three of the four other members of the Fight Back ticket for International office. Unlike some of the more outspoken progressive rank-and-file leaders who could be labeled as "radical" or "leftist" by the incumbent administration, staffpersons possessed an image of "responsible" union members who did not support "extremist" political views. Staff appointments, usually proposed by District Directors, were made by the International President himself, making it awkward for the incumbent administration or its endorsed candidates to condemn their own appointees as wild extremists out to destroy the USWA. Finally, Sadlowski felt that "rank-and-file groups had no place to go but to him" in the 1977 election (Barbero). Early in the campaign he concentrated on those in the union's political center because he felt that he already had the support of those on the left.

Each of these four explanations underlines how the Fight Back organizational structure and campaign strategy were molded by the broader union organizational environment. Official union networks were the major routes to political influence in the USWA, hence it was easier to follow them than it was to organize independent grassroots support. Second, one quality that made Sadlowski a desirable candidate was his past experience as both a local union official and as an International staff representative. Thus the process through which desirable candidates are "created" affects their political style. In this case, Sadlowski's experience as a staff representative predisposed him to use official structures, even when unofficial grassroots structures would have provided stronger support in the long run. Sadlowski's involvement in the union's politician-creating machine also caused him to accept the International leaders' concept of "legitimacy," i.e. the concept that staff representatives were more "responsible" and level-headed than rank-and-file activists. Fight Back was in the paradoxical position of playing the International's game in its selection of strategy, at the same time as it was emphasizing the grassroots orientation of its insurgent campaign platform.

In conforming to the International's political "rules," Fight Back was weakened. Even though its platform emphasized more grassroots input into union policy making, the activists shunned by the organization's pro-staff-representative strategy were less likely to commit much of their time to a campaign for a candidate who ostracized them. This was damaging since progressive rank-and-filers and their local networks included scores of union members who were experienced at organizing rallies, leafleting, and building political contacts in the face of organizational resistance. These were activities at which staff representatives were inexperienced or activities in which they were unable to engage because of their official positions.

Failure to Expand the Campaign to District Directorships

The delay in recognizing the shortcomings of its early strategy severely hampered Fight Back's strength. The reform group did not modify its strategy until four or five months prior to the election. This contributed to another major blunder of the campaign--not getting Fight Back candidates for District Director in most districts. It failed to build district organizations capable of campaigning for directorship nominations. These candidates would have been invaluable to the Fight Back effort. Sadlowski-backed district director candidates would have diverted McBride supporters attention from the Presidential race to contests in their own regions.* Moreover, if a District candidate did win, he could bolster the progressive block on the International Executive Board.[3] Given the fact that Sadlowski did win the majority of votes in ten Districts, it is highly likely that Fight Back could have gotten its candidates elected in five to ten Districts instead of the two it did win. If elected, Fight Back Directors could have helped consolidate progressive rank-and-file backing for local union slates as Sadlowski did himself in District 31 (Dowling). By building local support, such a District Director could have strengthened the progressive electoral base in subsequent International elections.

In addition, if a District Director candidate was recruited, nominated, and elected primarily through the efforts of the Fight Back organization, he or she would be more responsive than an independent candidate would be to future pressure from the rank-and-file organization. If Sadlowski hoped to nurture democracy in the USWA, he would have wanted to ensure that rank-and-filers had many voices at the International level. Such a bloc of supporters on the IEB would have been important to Sadlowski had he been elected. As C.L. Danzey, a chemist at the U.S. Steel Fairfield, Alabama Works remarked, Sadlowski "could have the best intentions in the world in Pittsburgh, but a few people down here that can't get their problems solved...are going to...blame Sadlowski even though" it might be the fault of the District Director. Therefore, he felt that any progressive President needed support from a number of friendly District Directors (Danzey).

MISREADING CHANGES IN THE INDUSTRIAL AND UNION ENVIRONMENT

The electoral failure of Fight Back cannot merely be explained by changes in the union or industrial environments. Rather, it was also the movement's *failure to recognize* those changes and its *failure to adapt its strategies* and political platform to those changes that weakened the movement. This was the same lag that had characterized previous rank-and-file movements. Fight Back's delay in recognizing the shortcomings of its centralized strategy restricted its ability to gain an understanding of what issues steelworkers outside Chicago and outside basic steel found important. For example, Fight Back was insensitive to regional issues such as the national autonomy issue in Canada and the open-shop issue in

---

* This tactic was used by Abel in 1965 to help keep McDonald supporters occupied with regional races, reducing their effectiveness as national campaigners (Herling 1972:140-41, 179-212).

the South.* Instead, Fight Back relied on issues that had been successfully used by past rank-and-file organizations, e.g. opposition to a dues increase, and on issues primarily pertaining to the basic steel industry, e.g. opposition to the Experimental Negotiating Agreement.

As a focus in their pre-election organizing, Fight Back selected the membership dues increase and International officers' salary hike as primary issues. However, this issue was a weak one. The dues increase might have cost some of the higher-paid workers $100 to $200 extra annually, but it was not the major concern of many rank-and-file workers. While Fight Back did indirectly point out the centralization of control in the union (by showing that the International leadership had orchestrated the increase at a convention that it "controlled"), it did not squarely address the issue of union democracy which was of interest to a broader segment of the union membership. To a steelworker from Buffalo--an area experiencing severe unemployment and stepped-up productivity pressures on those still on the job--the dues issue was unimportant:

> They might choose a safe issue like dues, although that's going to backfire on them too. A lot of locals are going broke [in the Buffalo area] and need more money. I don't think the steelworkers would mind paying a couple extra bucks if they got something for it [Berlin].

Ironically, Fight Back's decision to pursue the relatively weak dues rollback issue was a reaction to changes in the structure of the union and the economic climate of the early 1970s. With almost one-half of USWA membership outside basic steel, Fight Back was searching for an issue affecting *all* members. However, rather than spend the time to gain a more detailed understanding of the variety of issues important to different geographical and industrial groups, it relied on a "proven" strategy. Opposition to dues increases had been a traditional source of rank-and-file dissidence. Given Fight Back's limited contact with union members outside of basic steel, and hence their lack of understanding of what issues might be more salient to all union members, the dues issue was the logical choice for political focus. Also, Fight Back steered clear of any criticism of weak wage gains outside basic steel, because such a campaign issue would have pointed out the imbalance in wages between steelworkers and union members in other industries. This would not have endeared non-steelworkers to a movement emerging out of basic steel.

---

* For reasons stated earlier, I have not closely examined the role of Canadian Steelworkers here. A more detailed analysis is provided in my dissertation (Nyden 1979:252-89).

Without any carefully constructed list of specific union reforms affecting all union members, Fight Back leaders made generalizations from their own criticisms of the basic steel ENA. They argued that the ENA weakened the strength of the union by eliminating the union's right to strike. In the words of Jim Balanoff, giving up the "right to strike" in favor of binding arbitration was like "putting a watchdog in your house, and then telling everyone it has no teeth" (J. Balanoff). Based on this, Fight Back leaders argued that in all industrial workplaces represented by the USWA, there was a weakening of the union's power because of their "weak" image in basic steel. Oliver Montgomery, Fight Back's candidate for Vice President for Human Affairs, stated that the union must

> give the guy on the battle lines, the front lines in the mills, the kind of support he needs.... He must have power equal or greater than foremen in handling grievances.... He must have the right or a modified right to threaten [the company] with a strike.... This is the basic issue in this campaign, the solar plexus. Steelworkers need dignity on the job [Montgomery].[4]

However, it was unclear whether or not the right-to-strike issue always struck a responsive chord with union members outside of basic steel.

In any case, supporters were critical of the vague and general character of issues used in the campaign. Commenting on Sadlowski's discussion of the campaign issues, a Pittsburgh-area union member stated, "Concretely, he [Sadlowski] hasn't said that much" (McMills). Another active Fight Back campaigner in the Chicago area asserted that Sadlowski's campaign literature should have been "more hard-hitting and more specific, giving people a reason more than just being a new guy." He added that the insurgent did not "clearly take on the company or deal with issues such as racism, declining employment, and red-baiting of union dissidents" (Anonymous--Hammond). One Gary steelworker described Sadlowski as a "real liberal on the race issue," meaning that he opposed discrimination in principle, but did not firmly support any affirmative action program aimed at counteracting past discriminatory practices (Anonymous--Gary).*

---

* According to Jim Davis, leader of the Ad Hoc Commitee for Concerned Black Steelworkers--the only national black rank-and-file caucus--Sadlowski's attitude was relfected in the fact that he ignored Ad Hoc when early campaign strategies were being mapped (Davis).

Sadlowski ran a campaign calling on rank-and-filers to "trust" him to make reforms once he won office. This led John DelVecchio, a foundry worker and local union vice-president in Bridgeport, Connecticut, to remark that "Steelworkers Fight Back so far seems to be more like a campaign organization for Sadlowski, than the issue-raising organization" it had earlier claimed to be:[5]

> Sure, Sadlowski is going to need a lot of publicity and we're going to be pushing Sadlowski even if we don't agree with everything he says. He's certainly going to be the progressive candidate in the election. [However,] what we really want to see is a movement in the union. A movement doesn't really center around a person or around a president.... A movement centers around issues in the union [DelVecchio].

Election Results

Although receiving a higher proportion of the vote than prior challengers outside the USWA leadership, Fight Back candidates for the five top International offices fell short of victory. Sadlowski received 43.1 percent of the 578,142 votes cast (see Table 6.1).[6] The Fight Back candidate won majorities in ten of the twenty-five Districts. Given the campaign's focus on basic steelworkers in the industrial belt running from the Northeast through the Midwest, it was not surprising that all the districts won by Sadlowski were in this area (see Figure 6.1). He received the larger share of votes surrounding large industrial cities containing large basic steel plants--Baltimore, Bethlehem, Pittsburgh, Youngstown, Cleveland, Detroit, Chicago and Milwaukee.

Unionwide, Sadlowski received 51.9 percent of the votes from locals with 1,000 or more--locals predominantly in basic steel. However, he only won 37.6 percent of the ballots cast in the remaining smaller locals--locals predominantly outside of basic steel. Fight Back's strategy of concentrating its campaign efforts in large locals did not produce victory for two reasons. First, voter turnout in the large locals was not large enough to offset the votes cast by the small locals. Large locals contained 41 percent of the union's membership, but accounted for under 39 percent of the vote. A stronger showing in these locals would have been one way in which the rank-and-file movement could have compensated for the International's strength over the smaller locals--strength that the International had because these were largely non-steel locals and were locals more heavily influenced by International staff representatives due to their size.

Also, Lloyd McBride--the incumbent International leadership's choice for USWA President--succeeded in reducing potentially large Sadlowski pluralities in basic steel districts. McBride's hard campaigning in the Pittsburgh area, aided by a large number of friendly International staff representatives, held Sadlowski to only slight margins of victory in two Pittsburgh Districts (District 19 and 20) and dealt the Chicagoan a defeat in the third (District 15). In District 31, where Fight Back had hoped to win big to counterbalance losses elsewhere, the margin did not reach the 3:1 outcome expected by Fight Back.* Fight Back's particularly weak electoral showings in Canada (especially Quebec), in the South, and in locals outside basic steel were, in part, a product of its failure to appeal to diverse regional and industrial issues.** How these and other factors contributed to the decline of the rank-and-file movement in the late 1970s and early 1980s is discussed in the next chapter.

---

* This can be attributed to two factors. First, Fight Back's candidate for District Director was facing four other candidates who were supporting McBride. Consequently, McBride had extra "campaigners" on the District 31 ballot. Second, Fight Back had sent many of its District 31 supporters to other districts, reducing the number of campaigners who were available to get out the vote in Sadlowski's home district.

** Fight Back leaders claimed that vote stealing also accounted for the margin of defeat in Quebec and in some of the Districts in the South. While vote stealing may have taken place, it is unclear whether or not it would have reversed the election outcome. Fight Back lawyers were not successful in getting the courts to overturn the election on the basis of vote fraud.

Chapter 7

Decline in Industry and
Rank-and-File Movement
1979-Present

The late 1970s represented a watershed period in the evolution in steel industry structure, in the relationship between industry and union, and in the structure of the rank-and-file movement. While no new trends emerged, the continued development of trends first apparent in the early 1970s resulted in major changes in both industry and union. To steelworkers, 1979 was notable for one of the the largest declines in steel employment since the Depression. For the rank-and-file movement, the late 1970s and early 1980s represented a period of declining power; reform leaders who had been elected at the height of the rank-and-file insurgency were defeated and new attempts to influence union policy met with little success. Union strength in basic steel bargaining was undermined by the industry's increased ability to withstand union pressure. The newfound strength of steel corporations was a result of contraction, reduced dependency on union labor, ability to make profits at lower rates of capacity utilization, and major diversification moves which made corporations less dependent on steel production for their revenues.

THE INDUSTRY

Contemporary economic analyses of the American steel corporations have generally been a mixed bag in the early 1980s. On the one hand, recession, increased imports, declining sales, and plant shutdowns have all been components of a rather negative picture of the steel industry. On the other hand, the longterm prognosis for those companies surviving the contraction has been more positive. Nevertheless, the early 1980s has been a cloudy period for American steel companies. In late 1982 and early 1983, Bethlehem Steel discontinued its Lackawanna, New York operations, putting 7,300 employees out of work (*New York Times* 24 Jan. 1983). Other companies, such as U.S. Steel and Armco, are continuing to close sections of their plants. Still other steelmakers, such as McLouth Steel and National Steel, are declaring bankruptcy or trying to arrange employee buy-outs for their ailing operations. A further reflection of how strong an impact the early 1980s has had on the steel industry has been the reduction in dividends to stockholders and cutbacks on capital expenditures. Robert Levine, a credit ratings analyst, has observed that many steelmakers "have been paying dividends out of their capital base rather than their earnings base" (*Business Week* 9 Aug. 1982). In essence, the companies have been liquidating themselves. This has lead Peter Marcus, an analyst for Paine Webber Mitchel Hutchins, Inc., to conclude, "The question is not the steel companies' survivability; it is whether they can survive strong enough to benefit from the next recovery" (ibid.). However, what may be happening is a shake-out in the industry. Some companies are disappearing, others are paring back out-dated plants, and still others are continuing to diversify into non-steel areas.

For the survivors, this may mean an improved industry. Moreover, this improvement will be a product of trends initiated in the 1960s and early 1970s--contraction of the labor force, introduction of new technology, increased productivity, and elimination of inefficient plants. The changes in productivity sought by the industry's policies of the preceding two decades have already partially paid off in the 1980s. Between 1978 and the middle of 1981, the industry's workforce dropped by 11 percent while its shipments declined by only 3 percent. During the same period, overall profits increased from 2.8 percent to 4.3 percent of sales (although there have been some noticeable declines in the months following July 1981) (ibid. 12 Oct. 1981). Mini-mill corporation profits continued to average even higher, with most annual reported rates in the 14 to 30 percent range (*New York Times* 23 Sept.

1981). This is not to say that the industry is unaffected by recession--deepening economic problems have resulted in some moderation of these trends--but the industry is better prepared to withstand a downturn.

Perhaps one of the most significant changes in the industry has been its ability to be profitable at lower operating rates. *Business Week* (12 Oct. 1981) reports that the steel industry "is now finding that it can stay in the black while running at as little as 60 percent of capacity," even though as recently as 1978 it needed to run at 82 percent of capacity in order to break even (see also M. Brody 1981; *Wall Street Journal* 2 Nov. 1981). Also with increased product specialization by the larger integrated producers, the industry is working at maximizing its profits (*Business Week* 31 May 1982). Mini-mill corporations' reduced vulnerability to economic downturn--discussed in the preceding chapter--has certainly contributed to the industry's ability overall to cope with economic recession. This ability to operate at lower rates has been accompanied by a reduction in the industry's reliance on labor and has diminished its vulnerability to strikes.

The changing structure of the steel industry has also continued to weaken the role of organized labor. As the market share of large integrated mills has decreased, the share taken by mini-mills and foreign producers has continued to increase. Industry analysts believe that as early as 1986 mini-mills will account for 25 percent of American steel production (*New York Times* 23 Sept. 1981). Imports accounted for 16.3 percent of steel sold in the United States in 1980 (ibid. 6 Nov. 1981). In 1981, the proportion of imports rose to 23 percent of steel sales (*Business Week* 31 May 1982). This trend indicates a further weakening of the position of union steelworkers, who are concentrated in integrated steel mills.

Continuing diversification of the large integrated producers has also weakened the strength of organized labor in negotiations with the steel companies. The trends of the 1970s have continued into the 1980s. The 1982 U.S. Steel takeover of Marathon Oil has been the most dramatic step in steel corporation diversification. As a result of the $6.2 billion stock purchase, giving U.S. Steel a controlling interest in the oil company, steel will comprise less than 40 percent of U.S. Steel's total sales. In 1980 steel sales had comprised 70 percent of total sales for U.S. Steel (ibid. 7 Dec. 1981). Also in 1981, National Steel--the fourth-largest steel producer--purchased the fourth-largest savings and loan association in the United States through its United Financial Corporation subsidiary (M. Brody 1981). A year later, National Steel announced plans to sell off its 11,500-employee Weirton plant which represented one-third of its steel capacity (*Business Week* 15 March 1982). Armco has diversified to such an extent that it has now dropped the word "steel" from its corporate title (*New York Times* 23 Nov. 1981). To sum up the impact of changes in the American steel industry: an

upbeat long-term outlook for the industry has produced a
downbeat outlook for steelworkers. Diversification into
non-steel areas as well as the steel industry's ability to
survive periods of lower operating rates has reduced
vulnerability to union pressure. The power of the union at
the steel bargaining table has diminished. Moreover, hopes
among steelworker insurgents that the rank-and-file movement
will re-emerge without major changes in structure and strategy
have become false hopes, as they watch their traditional
supporters--basic steelworkers--dwindle in number.

THE UNION AND LABOR RELATIONS IN STEEL

Despite the dramatic decline in steel industry employment in
the late 1970s and early 1980s and the precipitous drop in
USWA membership to 600,000 in 1983, politically the
International union leadership has not been as seriously
affected by its shrinking constituency as one might think.
The employment decline in basic steel and other basic
industries represented by the USWA has been partially
compensated by the diversification of the union's membership
base which was taking place over the past decade. The top
officials have also benefited politically from the layoffs in basic
steel. Basic steel membership--long the center of
anti-International politics--has been decimated by plant
shutdowns and layoffs. A number of rank-and-file activists in
areas severely affected by plant shutdowns, e.g. Youngstown,
felt that the International did not fight very hard to prevent
the shutdowns. Helping basic steelworkers fight for their jobs
meant helping the opposition maintain the size of their ranks.
Symbolic of the International's victory over rank-and-file
dissidents in the wake of plant shutdowns was the elimination
of the USWA Youngstown District which had been one of the
strongholds of rank-and-file movements since the 1950s. The
District was ostensibly eliminated because of a loss of
membership due to steel plant shutdowns; but the fact that the
District was a longtime thorn in the side of the International
leadership certainly made the decision an easy one for top
USWA officials. This does not mean that the International did
not experience a loss in bargaining strength in basic steel. It
does mean that the trade off of bargaining strength for
reduced grassroots dissidence and greater political control over
the union was a trade off with which the International
leadership could live.
    In the wake of the major wave of job losses in steel the
leadership of the USWA has found itself in a weakened position
vis-a-vis steel management. From a 1974 production workforce
average size of 487,000, steel employment plummeted to 392,800
in 1980--a loss of more than 94,000 jobs in six years. Much of
the decline came with the large number of plant closings in
1979. More than 60 percent of the jobs lost in this six-year

period were lost in that one year.* Management has been using the continued threat of job eliminations both to win further cooperation from the top USWA leadership and to tame dissident rank-and-filers.   In this environment, where companies can now wrest concessions from the union, a *Barron's* article quoted one steel executive as "cheerfully" stating that the "closing of plants from here out is like cancer; it will be slow and painful, not quick and dirty" (M. Brody 1981).   This environment also affected union leaders. For example, in 1981, Jack Parton, who had just been elected Director of District 31, commented, "In every contract I'm called in to negotiate, the companies are saying, 'What can you give up to keep us from closing.'.... All you can do is hope the concessions will benefit the economy of the region" (*Local 1010 Steelworker* 1981).   "Givebacks" and "concessions" have become a regular part of USWA leadership's vocabulary in the 1980s.

Workers on the Defensive

Perhaps the most significant sign of modified union:management relations in this changed economic environment has been the failure of the two parties to renew the Experimental Negotiating Agreement which expired in 1980. Although the USWA and industry reached agreement on a national steel contract in 1980, the ENA was not renewed. Today, steel companies--less vulnerable to strikes because of automation as well as diversification--are not as anxious to "buy" industrial peace at as high a price as they were in the early 1970s when they were still reorganizing.   The ENA's exchange of a cost-of-living provision for a no-strike guarantee is no longer attractive to companies.   In fact, it is now the grassroots membership that wants the ENA's cost-of-living clause as protection against erosion of wages by inflation.   Unlike the early 1970s, when the ENA was the object of grassroots dissident criticism, the pact is now supported by most rank-and-filers.   In a 1981 membership referendum in District 31, union members supported the ENA by a 9:1 margin.   With workers on the defensive, the industry is in a position to make inroads in wages and workplace issues.

This is reflected in the 1980 national steel contract settlement.   The USWA failed to win its proposed provisions, such as clauses insuring job security, protection against plant

---

* The difference in the production workforce average size between 1979 and 1980 was 57,400.   Literally, this figure does not indicate only actual losses of jobs, it also includes temporary layoffs.   However, given the permanent nature of steel industry contraction, many of these "temporary" layoffs will become permanent.   Therefore, this is an approximation of actual job losses.

shutdowns, guarantees for a shorter work week, improved health and safety regulations, and a stronger grievance system (*In These Times* 1980). Instead the union made major concessions. It gave up a demand for increased pensions. Its wage gains were modest, even by industry standards. The union also agreed to study the existing bargaining structure and possibly split up different sectors of the industry and bargain separately. If a split ultimately takes place it would weaken union influence over the industry, since one group of workers could then be played off against against another. In an article entitled "The Steel Labor Agreement: A Better Deal for Industry Than It Appears," *Dun's Review* reporter Arnold R. Weber says of the 1980 negotiations:

> It was apparent...that one of the longest recorded honeymoons since Queen Victoria and Prince Albert was coming to a close. The companies did not seek to reverse previous gains but pressed successfully several modifications of principles.... [The contract settlement signaled] the triumph of economic realism over expediency and tradition [1980].

The end of the honeymoon has also been apparent in the negotiating process for the 1983 basic steel agreement. Although incumbent USWA President Lloyd McBride has been characterized as a pro-concessions negotiator, a first effort at an early contract settlement failed in July 1982 when the union leader recommended that the Basic Steel Industry Conference (BSIC)--a group of 400 local union presidents from basic steel locals--reject the steel industry's contract proposal. A second tentative agreement between the International leadership and the industry in November 1982 was rejected by the BSIC over McBride's objections. The rejection of the November agreement was an unusual show of dissension by the local union presidents. It was an indicator of the continued existence of some rank-and-file reform sentiment at the local level. However, rather than interpreting this as a rejuvenation of the movement, it may be more easily seen as the gasps of a movement struggling to keep alive.

The 1983 contract was finally approved by the BSIC on March 1 by a vote of 169 to 83--five months before contract expiry. The contract included concessions ranging from an average 9 percent cut in workers' pay in the first year to reduction in some benefits (*Business Week* 14 March 1983; *New York Times* 2 March 1983). The steel companies used the sagging steel market and plant closings as justifications for the wage cutbacks and other concessions. Some industry observers have argued that the concessions have come just before a period in which industry expects an upturn. According to the *Wall Street Journal*, some analysts have suggested that "the new pact represents the last chance steelworkers had to argue poor financial health in seeking concessions before a steel recovery begins" (2 March 1983).*

Labor-Management Participation Teams

One provision of the 1980 contract was the establishment of "labor-management participation teams" to improve productivity in the steel mills. While the teams have not become widespread, they represent a changing orientation to workplace management. The teams resemble "Quality Circles" (QCs) which are becoming increasingly popular with American management. The USWA-steel industry teams consist of ten to fifteen rank-and-file workers and supervisors at the departmental level. The teams will seek

> to solve problems that are not addressed in the traditional union-management procedure. The teams will give workers a chance to deal with problems such as production bottlenecks, safety and health issues, the efficient use of tools, absenteeism, incentive pay, product quality, and other knowledge [*Business Week* 29 June 1981].

While industry spokespersons describe their teams as marking progress in union:management relations, the quality circle concept represents a further erosion of union influence in the workplace and an increase in management control over the work process. By dealing with worker:management disagreements, QCs begin to supplant the existing grievance system. While existing grievance procedure rules are explicitly defined by the contract, quality circles have few explicit guidelines. Rather than resolve new problems in labor relations through changes in contract language or its interpretation, quality circles may increasingly supplant the traditional mode of union:management conflict resolution. QCs are more likely to come up with ad hoc solutions than well-defined precedents binding both parties in subsequent conflicts.

Where the industrial relations system had once worked to bureaucratize the union:management relationship, quality circles introduce a social process which resolves problems as they arise, without building an elaborate set of written labor relations rules. Quality circles introduce "uncertainty" where once there had been "certainty." Organizational sociologists

---

* Prior to the concessions of the 1983 contract, union and management did experiment with other techniques of increasing labor productivity and reducing labor costs. The 1980 contract had opened the door for the introduction of "labor-management participation teams" in selected steel plants. Although this program never took hold, it is useful to examine the implications of such attempts at changing the traditional union:management workplace relationship.

have pointed out that managers, who are given greater latitude over decision making in areas of "uncertainty," generally become more powerful in the organization (J. Pfeffer 1978). Thus, any increased use of quality circles would increase the QC's influence over the workplace and reduce the role of the existing union:management grievance system.

Moreover, because management tends to dominate quality circles, adoption of quality circles would enhance management shopfloor control and further erode union power in the workplace. In his extensive analysis of Japanese quality circles--the model for most recent American plans--Robert Cole found that QCs represent a method of better integrating foremen and supervisers into the shopfloor work process. Foremen are often marginal personnel. On the one hand, they are not perceived as full-fledged members of management. On the other hand, they are not seen as part of the rank-and-file work groups from which they are usually recruited. However, QCs systematically integrate foremen into production-level social organization. Foremen become key actors in quality circles. Through QCs they come to supplant the informal leaders that emerge out of groups of production workers on the shopfloor. Cole notes that many researchers "see QC circles as a device to break worker collective resistance and rebuild group solidarity on the basis of mangement goals" (1980:203).

On another level, the "labor-management participation teams" represent a further rationalization of the work process and increased management control over shopfloor decision making. This process started with the abolition of craft worker control in the 1890s and continued with the introduction of scientific management principles in the early twentieth century. In *Labor and Monopoly Capital,* Harry Braverman points out that management practices in the early twentieth century were geared toward separating the "conception" of work from the "execution" of work (1974). By studying the workplace and instituting more controlled and detailed production systems, managers were taking more control over the decision-making, the shopfloor judgments, and the "creativity" involved in production. Workers increasingly only carried out the orders of management; the shopfloor employee was primarily involved in executing a pre-existing production plan.

In a sense, quality circles represent a bold management strategy to gain even more control over the production process. It is an effort to dig even deeper into the rank-and-file worker's mind and extract what conceptual or creative processes he or she still controls. Even where conception and execution have ostensibly been separated, workers familiar with the day-to-day aspects of production are still quite aware of the flaws in the production process--bottlenecks in the efficient flow of the factory. Bottlenecks may result from inappropriately designed machinery; they may also be the products of poorly organized social structures in the workplace which hinder high productivity because of poor communication or the interpersonal tension which results. One goal of QCs is to increase worker identification with the company--to make the worker feel that he is a partner in management. In this atmosphere it is expected that workers will be more willing to help the company in pinpointing and resolving shopfloor problems. Specifically referring to the new teams in the steel industry, *Business Week* remarked that they are "efforts to tap rank-and-file knowledge" (29 June 1981). In their analysis of autoworkers' experience with QCs, Mike Parker and Dwight Hansen--two United Auto Workers union members--observe that

> Quality Circles become a Junior Achievement-style management training ground where people learn to think and act like managers. The more advanced QWL [Quality of Work Life] programs are explicitly organized so that in the words of the former GM director of organizational development, "each team is like a small business" [1983:35].

One union leader put it differently, saying that QCs are "a company ball game, with company umpires, on company turf" (ibid.)

Quality of worklife programs are not inherently attractive to rank-and-filers. However, they are usually presented as painless ways of improving productivity and hence a way of achieving more stable wages and job security in a period of industrial contraction and high unemployment. Writing in 1983, Parker and Hansen quip that "QWL is a sort of union version of Reaganomics: Help the company make more profits so that some of the wealth will trickle down in the form of more jobs" (ibid.:34).

The bottom line is that QCs are an inexpensive way of increasing worker productivity. The *New York Times* notes that implementation of quality circles "does not require large amounts of capital, and it fits in with the strategy of squeezing more production out of older plants" (25 May 1981). In the context of neo-Marxist theory which argues that industry is perpetually trying to gain ground in the "contested terrain" of the workplace by gaining control over workplace knowledge, this development in the steel industry is quite significant. Management is trying to push further into the workplace "terrain."

It should be noted that in the recent period of increased union:management conflict over collective bargaining, the International leadership has been less supportive of the quality circles negotiated in the 1980 agreement. However, this does not mean that management will abandon its efforts, particularly as more and more American companies use elements of this new management technique.

THE RANK-AND-FILE MOVEMENT: ONCE AGAIN SLOW TO ADAPT

When asked how strong the rank-and-file movement was in 1981, a steelworker who had been active in local, district, and unionwide reform movements commented, "If you're looking for a rank-and-file movement today, you'll need a magnifying glass" (Anonymous--Gary). The absence of any ongoing regional or national rank-and-file reform organizations in the USWA supports this observation. In 1981 USWA elections, the top five incumbent International officials were not challenged by any reform candidates. Only a loosely connected group of five District Director candidates made the effort to challenge the incumbent USWA administration. The "alliance" between candiates running in the Chicago, North Central, Pittsburgh, Ontario, and Northern Ohio districts--Districts 31, 33, 15, 6, and 27, respectively--involved joint press conferences where the candidates stated their support for some general principles. The principles included adoption of a more aggressive bargaining stance toward industry, an equitable dues structure, the right to ratify contracts, and less International union "interference" in union elections. With the exception of the campaign organizations that were active within the respective districts, no unionwide rank-and-file organization existed.

Of the five candidates only one--Dave Patterson in the Ontario district--was victorious. Jim Balanoff, Sadlowski's close political ally who had won the District Directorship in 1977, was narrowly defeated by a pro-International candidate in the Chicago district. Reflecting on his loss and on the general weakness of the rank-and-file movement, Balanoff observed, "Our mistake in '77 was that Steelworkers Fight Back didn't stay alive. You need an organization. I don't think the losses would have occurred if Fight Back had stayed alive" (*In These Times* 1981). While this observation correctly points to the lack of any unionwide organization as a shortcoming of the rank-and-file movement, it does not recognize the flaws of a Fight Back style organization, i.e. its concentration in basic steel, its lack of broad-based grassroots participation, and its vague political ideology. It also does not recognize that there have been changes in both steel industry employment patterns and in union membership characteristics. However, it should be noted that Balanoff's ability to win almost 50 percent of the vote represents an improvement over 1977 when he received only 40 percent of the vote--which was all he needed to win in the three-way race that year. Nevertheless, if it is to regain strength the rank-and-file movement will have to make major adjustments in strategy to deal with recent changes in the industry and in the union.

The movement's traditional source of support--basic steelworkers--has been undermined by industrial contraction. Moreover, those steelworkers still working have been shaken by the plant closings and extensive layoffs around them.

Rank-and-file steelworkers are now more concerned with *preserving* their past gains in contract bargaining than they are with embarking on major challenges to the industry or union leadership.   Rank-and-file leaders themselves recognize this.   Explaining why he voted to ratify the 1980 steel industry contract, Balanoff expressed his ambivalence and frustration: "It addresses what annoyed us. Could we have done better? I don't know.   Here you have only two choices--take this or arbitration. Would I take this instead of a strike?   I don't know" (*In These Times* 1980).   Rudy Schneider, a long-time activist at Local 1010, admitted, "They got a better agreement than I figured they would" (ibid.). This reaction to the 1980 contract, the failure in the 1981 elections, and the lack of any visible rank-and-file reform organization raise the question whether or not a rank-and-file movement can re-emerge in the USWA.   This issue is discussed in the last chapter, along with some further analysis of the social and economic factors that have affected the movement over the past four decades.

Chapter 8

Conclusions: The Past, Present and Future of the Movement

There are elements in the social environment that are beyond the control of individuals or of social movements--elements which can shape the behavior of individuals and development of social movements. At the same time, there are organizational structures and strategies which can be controlled by individuals or social movement leaders--structures and strategies which can influence reform movement development. I have tried to outline both the factors which can limit union reform activity and those activities which can circumvent or overcome some of these limitations. Because the last period covered in this book has been one characterized by industrial decline in the steel industry, the present study is particuarly useful in understanding the impact that permanent contraction will have on other segments of American industry experiencing similar changes. Specifically, it is helpful in understanding the future of workplace politics, rank-and-file reform movements, and the American union movement in general. Currently, the American union movement is experiencing a decline in membership, weakened strength vis-a-vis business in collective bargaining, and reduced political strength.

First, this final chapter will discuss the evolving relationship between rank-and-file movement, union, and industry. The theoretical implications of the study will be discussed here. Second, it will look at the future of rank-and-file movements in general, i.e. rank-and-file movements in any union. Because one cannot separate reform movements from the organizations they are seeking to reform, I really will be examining the future of union organizations themselves. Possible paths that labor organizations may follow in dealing with both their diminishing strength and the economic and social crises of the 1980s will be outlined here. Third, in particular, the final section of the chapter will examine the effectiveness of different paths that union leaders and rank-and-file organizations might take in dealing with the crises.

THE POLITICAL ECONOMY OF RANK-AND-FILE MOVEMENT DEVELOPMENT

Like most unions, the early years of the USWA were characterized by an adversarial relationship with industry. While the present study argues that unionization was ultimately functional for the industry's economic stability, this was not necessarily management's view when it was first confronted with union organizers. In these early years, rank-and-file workers played a major role in organizing the union--either through direct involvement as organizers or through generalized resistance to management practices on the shopfloor. Rank-and-file militancy contributed to the adversarial union:management relationship in the early years. Because grassroots militants were an integral part of the early union and because the union was satisfying many rank-and-filers' expectations regarding wage gains and improved working conditions, there was not a noticeable separation between the "rank and file" and the union administration. There was not a distinct rank-and-file movement. However, by the late 1940s, such a movement did emerge in reaction both to centralization of union decision-making and to fears that moderation of the union's adversarial stance vis-a-vis industry management would mean more limited gains in working conditions and wages.

Leadership Centralization and Extra-organizational Factors

Contrary to organizational theories attempting to explain oligarchy and leadership centralization as a natural intra-organizational maturation process, one must examine leadership centralization--and the emergence of a rank-and-file movement in reaction to it--in a broader context. In the case of the present study, changes in the overall society and in the industry itself contributed to leadership centralization and its integration into the industrial relations process. The character of the broader social, political, and economic environments provided the pressures causing centralization of policy-making functions within the union.

In retrospect, it is apparent that unions are functional in modern capitalist society insofar as they provide another layer of social control. Unions are organizations which can channel grassroots activity away from demands potentially damaging to management control, e.g. demands for a greater worker role in shopfloor decision making, and toward less threatening demands, e.g. demands for improved wages and benefits which can be compensated for by higher prices and increased productivity. However, at the same time as dominant social institutions pull union leaders away from rank-and-file interests and toward corporate interests, this cooptation process creates disenchantment among grassroots workers. Pre-union disenchantment leads to a union movement; disenchantment after a union is established produces an internal rank-and-file movement.

Lag in Social Movement Adaptability

However, like the original union movement, this new rank-and-file movement is not entirely the product of conscious activity by reformers. Examination of the early rank-and-file movement in the Steelworkers union shows that the movement is influenced by the same organizational, political, economic, and social forces which influence incumbent union leaders. Given the similarity of the USWA to other unions--in terms of its history, structure, and relationship to industry--this phenomenon is likely to be present in rank-and-file movements in other unions. Throughout its history, the Steelworkers rank-and-file reform movement has had local shopfloor networks as its basic building blocks. Given the limited resources of any budding social movement--and the difficulty of functioning at broad regional, national, or international levels--it is likely that initial activity will be restricted to the local level. At the same time, the perceptions of an emerging social movement are affected by its position in the social process. This has meant that for much of its history, the rank-and-file movement has viewed local issues or single-industry issues as more important than unionwide issues or broad worker rights issues. In the early years of the union, this orientation was further encouraged by localized collective bargaining and decentralized control of shopfloor practices.

However, in the late 1940s, as industrial structure and union structure became more centralized, the movement did not adjust its strategies and tactics accordingly. It did not change its focus to industrywide or unionwide levels. This change did not occur for a number of reasons. First, there is a built-in lag in the speed of reaction of a social movement to changes in its social environment. A movement may emerge at one time because it is reacting to a specific set of grievances. Its ideology and its strategies are formed in reaction to these grievances and to elements of the social environment which stimulated those grievances. However, because social movements are often quite decentralized, they do not always react quickly to changes in their environment. If changes in the environment at a later time stimulate new and different grievances, social movements which have developed ideologies and strategies around older grievances do not necessarily have the self-regulating capacities to adjust quickly to changes in the political, economic, or social environments. As suggested in the social movement literature, without the institutionalization of the movement into a structured organization, the movement remains amorphous. In this amorphous stage--when it is at best a loose coalition of local networks--it does not have the capacity to consciously evaluate changes in the environment; nor does it have the capacity to devise strategies of reacting to those changes in order to maintain or increase movement strength. Thus, there is often a time lag between changes in the environment and the adjustment of the movement's ideology and strategy to those changes.

Ameliorative Measures Inhibiting Social Movement Growth

Social forces inhibiting movement development also may undermine the movement by removing some of the original sources of disenchantment. In the case of the Steelworkers rank-and-file movement, the wage improvements of the 1940s, 1950s, and 1970s, as well as the management concession providing for limited local autonomy in the 1940s and 1950s, were ameliorative measures used to cool down and distract the emerging rank-and-file movement. As a consequence of the provision for limited local autonomy, what rank-and-file disenchantment did exist was focused at local levels. Time was not spent on organizing and maintaining a unionwide movement organization. The industry could afford the real wage increases and could compensate for any productivity loss due to limitations in workplace control because it could fall back on the expanding economy of the era after World War II. Similarly, the top union leaders who "won" those gains for union members were able to do so because of the industry's ability to pay the price.

Industrial Austerity and Grassroots Disenchantment

When this steel industry prosperity of the 1950s--which was largely a product of expansion in the overall economy--disappeared in the 1960s, significant changes occurred in the industry:union:rank-and-file movement relationship. These changes in the steel industry economy reflected not only changes in the broader economy, but reflected structural changes in the industry. Specifically, years of making profits by riding the wave of the expanding economy, without significant new investment, started to hurt the industry. Steel produced by newer, more efficient foreign producers started to push American steel products out of both the foreign and domestic markets. More efficient mini-mills started to sprout up in the United States and grew by leaps and bounds in the 1970s. These changes pressured integrated producers to restructure steel production and change industrial relations policies. These changes ultimately affected the Steelworkers union and the rank-and-file movement.

The reorganization of the steel industry, started in the early 1960s, involved real wage stabilization and increased management control over the workplace. This, in turn, enabled the industry to embark on automation of steel facilities, elimination of inefficient plants, and diversification of investments into non-steel enterprises. While the fruits of these projects were not harvested until the early 1980s, planning for them was initiated after the 1959 strike. Attainment of stabilized labor costs and increased management control over the workplace required the cooperation of the union. Given past cooperation between industry leaders and top union officials, the groundwork for this process had been established. Increased centralization of union decision making would further insulate the industrial relations process from any disruption by grassroots dissidents--dissidents who had been unsuccessful in unionwide electoral challenges in the 1950s, but who nevertheless could potentially disrupt industrial relations. Thus, the 1960s and 1970s were decades characterized by an International union leadership offensive to consolidate power within the union.

Using the collective bargaining process which had grown increasingly centralized in the 1950s, industry and top union leaders agreed to limited wage increases and elimination of local control over workplace practices. In cooperating with the industry, International union leaders felt confident that their political control over the union organization would not be threatened. Not only had their internal power been strengthened over the first two decades of the union, but the rank-and-file movement was weak at the unionwide level. Years of pursuing local issues and organizing local networks, instead of concentrating on national issues and organizing unionwide coalitions, had caused the rank-and-file movement to remain weak vis-a-vis the International leadership.

Transformation of Militancy into Organized Insurgency

Conditions present in the 1960s led to increased disenchantment among rank-and-file steelworkers. In contract settlements the International leadership agreed to eliminate local autonomy and stabilize real wages. This increased membership disenchantment with the union leadership. While some rank-and-file dissatisfaction with the level of shopfloor control exists in any industrial setting, the absence of compensatory rewards, such as increased real wages, can accentuate the feeling of powerlessness among rank-and-file workers. However, this is not necessarily translated into visible, organized reform activity. The extent to which disenchantment is transformed into organized insurgency is related to a number of factors. The social structure of the workplace, and the degree to which it facilitates the emergence of a rank-and-file leadership capable of articulating issues and convincing workers to support changes, are basic elements in the transformation of generalized militancy into social movement organizations. The political consciousness of those leaders, their selection of issues, and the structures and strategies of grassroots organizations affect the ability of a movement to grow stronger. Many of these factors are within the control of rank-and-file reformers; however, there are other broader social, political, and economic processes which influence their choices. The legal system, political traditions, media, past industrial relations practices, and even the geographical distribution of industry all influence the development of the rank-and-file movement. Minor organizational reforms or changes in leadership personalities can also temporarily ameliorate grassroots disenchantment and temporarily sidetrack the rank-and-file movement. This was the case with the replacement of incumbent USWA President David McDonald with USWA Secretary-Treasurer I.W. Abel in the 1965 International elections.

Reducing Grassroots Disenchantment

However, by the late 1960s and early 1970s, the reform movement once again gained strength. The quieting effect that a leadership change and limited union reforms had had on rank-and-file activity was wearing off. Still, neither the industry nor the union could afford a major rank-and-file insurgency at this time. The industry was continuing its restructuring program and it was not complete. The union leadership was bolstering its centralized control through membership diversification, and it was not yet clear if it could withstand a well-organized grassroots challenge centered in a shrinking, but still large, basic steel membership.

With more time and further membership diversification, the International leadership could play off various sectors of industrial membership against one another. This would insulate it from the traditional dominance of basic steelworkers in union elections and policy-making. Furthermore, the USWA leadership undoubtedly saw the handwriting on the wall; as a result of industry restructuring, basic steel employment ultimately was going to drop drastically in the near future. Given the likelihood that declines in basic steel industry employment and diversification of union membership would undermine dissident political strength in the long run, there was no desire by either the industry or the top union leadership to precipitate a major confrontation at this time. Therefore, the proven tactic of providing real wage increases to quiet the rank-and-file was again used in the early 1970s to take some of the wind out of the insurgent movement's sails. The Experimental Negotiating Agreement brought substantial wage increases as well as a guarantee of steady industrial production. In essence, the ENA bought time for the industry and top union leadership.

However, despite these ameliorative measures, the rank-and-file movement did continue to gain strength, based on the lingering reaction to the lack of real wage increases and declining workplace conditions experienced in the previous ten years. Although rank-and-file movement organizations of the 1970s--particularly Steelworkers Fight Back--adopted some unionwide organizing strategies and were clearly stronger than previous insurgent organizations, they ultimately failed to achieve major unionwide political power by the end of the decade. The failure was a product of problems in the movement's internal structure and strategy as well as a product of broader environmental factors which impinged on the movement's ability to fully develop.

FAILURE OF THE 1970S RANK-AND-FILE MOVEMENT

The decline of the rank-and-file reform movement--marked by the failure of Steelworkers Fight Back in 1977 and the decline in rank-and-file activity in subsequent years--is attributable to both the combination of economic, social, and political processes beyond the control of movement organizations and to the weaknesses in rank-and-file organization strategy and structure. First, let us examine the broader environmental factors influencing the movement.

Basic steel employment has declined, undermining the movement by destroying its traditional constituency. Also the union membership is more diversified, making it more difficult to construct a political strategy capable of bridging a large variety of issues important to members spread over a wide geographical area and employed in a wide variety of industries. The centralization of union decision-making and collective bargaining functions has made it more difficult to challenge the top leadership or influence industrial relations. The general economy itself has been in decline, causing some workers to be more hesitant in criticizing the union leadership in a time of crisis.

Broader, and sometimes more subtle, influences of American values and social institutions have also affected the character of the rank-and-file movement and its ability to grow. Many of these influences do not represent insurmountable obstacles to a rank-and-file movement, but nevertheless are formidable obstacles as long as rank-and-file leaders succumb to their influence. For example, reliance on legal strategies--e.g. suing to overturn elections and seeking injunctions against incumbents' use of union newspapers for electioneering--as a source of publicity and political strength has distracted movement organizations from the basic task of organizing grassroots support networks. Similarly, the use of legitimate channels within the union, e.g. Fight Back's use of staff representatives as candidates and political allies, has distracted contemporary groups from building an independent grassroots political base.

Appeal of Media and Legal Strategies

The movement's use of the media and legal institutions also illustrates the way in which a movement is affected by a strategy of using legitimizing institutions as sources of political strength in the place of grassroots organizing. Reliance on the media as a way of communicating with potential supporters and reliance on legal institutions as sources of political strength stunt long term movement growth by producing movement leaders and organizations with underdeveloped ties to their constituency. It also influences the character of the movement. First, reliance on media coverage results in an emphasis on leadership *personalities* rather than a focus on movement *ideology*. American politics emphasizes the personality of political leaders, and the media reflect this emphasis. In using the media, movement organizations tend to abandon issues, e.g. the improvement of workplace safety, establishment of greater employment stability, and elimination of racial discrimination. Instead, they emphasize leadership style, e.g. stress that a reform leader is "honest," "one of the boys," or "a fighter."

In the process of "making" the news, the media tend both to discard the more complex political issues and to avoid any elaborate analysis of the social movement organization.[1] Instead, the media artifically elevate individual leaders to prominent postions. This is done because the media (1) have limited time and space in which to cover the news, and (2) are trying to communicate to a broad audience. Individuals are easier to interview than entire movements or organizations. Individuals and their political statements are also more easily described and analyzed. Because the media are communicating to a general audience, media reports provide only a simplified picture of a movement which may not accurately convey a movement's goals to potential constituents. When newspaper reporters or television newscasters report developments in the union, their intent is not to provide an elaborate analysis of

workplace politics.   Rather, they are communicating a general
description of an event to a general audience.   This is another
reason why focusing on movement leaders is an attractive
reporting technique in the media.   By focusing on movement
leaders--as was the case with the media's attraction to
Sadlowski--the media find it easier to communicate a story to
the public than they do if they provide a more in-depth
analysis of movement goals.   In accommodating these practices,
movement organizations tend to adopt an emphasis on
leadership personalities rather than ideology.

Also, the Steelworkers rank-and-file movement shied away
from tactics or ideologies which might be viewed as radical by
the media and thus not legitimate for media coverage.   Even
though there might have been a socialist undercurrent to
recent rank-and-file movement organizations, i.e. in the way
that some rank-and-file groups have questioned management's
rights to determine workplace practices and to lay off workers,
this has not been emphasized.   Movement organizations have
not stressed these issues and the media generally have not
covered them.   The combined effect has been to water down
the existing political ideology of the movement and inhibit any
radicalization of its political view.   Thus, by accepting media
coverage as a major way of communicating with its
constituents--a tempting strategy given the massive size and
scope of the constituency--the movement is itself affected by
the limitations inherent in media coverage.

Inappropriate Strategies

Finally, there are more conscious choices that recent
movement leaders have made, which have led to the
deterioration of the movement.   By focusing its unionwide
organizing on basic steel, as well as by relying heavily on
contacts from past rank-and-file campaigns, recent
rank-and-file organizations--most notably Steelworkers Fight
Back--have incorporated a flaw into their strategies.   They
have not recognized that basic steel membership has shrunk
since the 1957 and 1969 campaigns; they have not recognized
that traditional sources of support have to be supplemented by
substantial political campaigning in other industrial and
geographic sectors of the membership.   This shows why social
movement organizations do not quickly adapt their strategies to
changes in the environment.   Movement organizations that have
growing, but still limited, resources generally do not have the
luxury of spending time to re-examine the strengths and
weaknesses of past strategies.   A lag gets built into
organizing tactics.

The need to build grassroots support by the quickest
available means can lead to still other movement organization
weaknesses.   In the case of Fight Back, the adoption of a
centralized structure--an efficient but somewhat "undemocratic"
strategy--alienated a large number of grassroots activists.
Many of these activists would have been willing to work hard

if they had thought they would have some say over organizational policies and possibly some political power if the insurgent organization was victorious. Also, the centralized campaign cut off lines of communication with supporters outside of basic steel and outside of Chicago who could have advised Fight Back on strategies and issues which were most important in their industries or regions. Instead, the Chicago- and steel-dominated leadership adopted a more parochial set of issues. It is important to understand that this centralized structure was not the result of *consolidation of power* by a leadership clique within a organization. Rather, it was the result of a local, informal social network's attempting to *build an organization around itself.*

In the absence of unionwide grassroots support-building, Fight Back did not even adopt the middle-of-the-road strategy available to them--building support in selected regions by running candidates for district offices. In its rush to win the top International office, Fight Back failed to build networks at either local or regional levels. Had district candidates been supported by Fight Back in its centers of support, i.e. the remaining pockets of basic steel strength in Pittsburgh, Youngstown, Cleveland, Baltimore, Bethlehem, Detroit, and Milwaukee, the rank-and-file movement would have been able to elect a number of supporters on the International Executive Board--the major unionwide policy-making body. While this would not have necessarily reversed the decline of the movement today, it may have slowed it down and may have kept it more visible. Moreover, it might have provided a foundation for a broader-based movement which could have more ably addressed the serious issues of job loss and plant shutdowns that now plague the industry.

FUTURE OF THE MOVEMENT

A number of factors have to be considered in order to understand the future of the rank-and-file movement in the USWA--or for that matter, the future of rank-and-file movements in other American unions. First, as already indicated, the state of the economy has weakened the movement in the Steelworkers union and most likely has weakened movements in other unions. However, this does not mean that the movement is dead. In both the 1930s and 1970s, workers' movements emerged after periods of inactivity or after periods characterized by relative powerlessness among rank-and-file workers. In the 1930s, it led to the formation of the union; in the 1970s it led to the growth of rank-and-file insurgency. Also in both cases, the rise in grassroots social activity occurred as wages and conditions were improving after a prolonged period of decline or limited gain. This suggests that rank-and-file activity may increase once the economic restructuring now occurring is fully institutionalized. The stabilization of industrial employment levels and improved or stabilized real wages that may result may set the scene for a renewed insurgency.

However, the fundamental structural changes in both industry and union indicate that a re-emergence in grassroots militancy would not necessarily be transformed into a rejuvenation of an organized reform movement. The movement's ability to adopt radically different strategies and ideas would be a crucial variable in translating militancy into successful reform activity. Indeed, given the current restructuring of the American economy and the declining power of unions, one might ask if unions themselves will survive in the restructured economy unless they too adopt radically new strategies and ideas. Thus, an analysis of the future of the progressive grassroots worker movement--inside and outside the Steelworkers union--must be an analysis of the union itself.

Specifically, the "intra-organizational adaptive" strategies that have been used by top USWA leaders and by leaders of other unions faced with declining membership in key sectors, e.g. diversification of membership, union merger, and leadership centralization to better control dissidence, are strategies that ultimately will fail to maintain union strength. On the other hand, the more innovative "extra-organizational adaptive" strategies increasingly supported by the rank-and-file activists who do remain, e.g. forming alliances with community groups and other interest groups adversely affected by industrial decline and present corporate policies, have a greater potential for maintaining or increasing union strength. The differences between these intra-organizational and extra-organizational strategies are described later in this chapter. I will argue that the current intra-organizational strategies followed by union leaders will ultimately fail, weakening their political strength vis-a-vis the strength of the rank-and-file movement which still exists, despite its low ebb. The key questions will be: (1) what factors would cause the progressive rank-and-file movement to piece itself back together and (2) will the union movement be fundamentally weakened before a rank-and-file movement re-emerges?

ORGANIZATIONAL STRATEGIES AVAILABLE TO UNIONS

Labor organizations have two potential avenues to follow in responding to the present threat to unionized labor. One response--an intra-organizational adaptive strategy--is the modification of union organizational structure to insulate the organization from shifts in economic structure. As demonstrated by the case study of the USWA, diversification of the membership base as a means of reducing vulnerability to workforce contraction in any one industry is a major intra-organizational strategy used by unions today. It provides "membership insurance" for the union, guaranteeing that it will not be severely weakened by employment declines in any one industry. Diversification can be achieved through mergers with smaller unions or through selective organizing drives--particularly in areas where the labor force is growing. This strategy increases the strength of the organization by increasing its *internal* resources--new members and the dues they pay.

Distinct from this *intra*-organizational survival strategy is an *inter*-organizational (or extra-organizational) strategy. This latter strategy broadens an organization's resource base by seeking greater cooperation with other organizations having similar political and economic interests. The improved resource base may include (1) support from a larger number of people, (2) increased political leverage, or (3) improved financial resources. Resources obtained through inter-organizational linkages might increase the power of unions, vis-a-vis large corporations. For example, unions closely aligned with non-labor organizations, such as community, religious, and small business groups, might be able to stave off plant shutdowns or at least might be able to modify corporate policy in communities negatively affected by changing economic structure. Such coalitions could slow down the process of domestic industrial contraction, or at least could hold corporations more accountable to workers and community residents. Participation in political coalitions where labor might become more involved in domestic and foreign policy issues, e.g. equal rights, nuclear disarmament, or changes in military aid policies, could provide reciprocal support for "labor issues" at a future date.

Stopping the Decline: The Top Leadership's Perspective

Union leaders are most likely to seek the avenue which maintains or improves their control over the organization. The impact on the membership and the overall labor movement are secondary considerations. Thus, from the perspective of union leaders, intra-organizational survival strategies are most appealing. Unlike inter-organizational alliances, intra-organizational strategies do not require give and take on the part of the leadership. They are aimed at increasing internal organizational resources without altering the existing mechanisms of control over those resources. Specifically, the expansion of the membership--through mergers or organizing drives--brings new resources into the union (dues and members), but does not change policy-making mechanisms. Pockets of new members do not represent competing power centers; they represent new resources.

Moreover, if the membership becomes more diversified in this process (diversified in terms of occupational, industrial, and geographical characteristics), the power of incumbent union leaders is futher enhanced. In fact, the power enhancement may take place even when membership expansion has not been achieved, but rather when stabilization or slight decline in membership has occurred. While recruitment increases the *size of* the membership base from which the leader derives his power, diversification consolidates the leader's *power over* that membership base--power that can increase despite a limited drop in membership size. Because a homogeneous membership is more likely to produce rank-and-file challenges to union leaders, the cultivation of heterogeneity among the membership reduces the possibility that anti-incumbent political groups will emerge, or, emerging, be successful. Diversification limits the opportunities for membership cooperation at grassroots levels. It reduces the possibility that a cluster of large locals or members of a large industrial conference within the union will provide the base for political opposition to incumbent national or international union leaders.

Because of the relatively lower costs of diversification through mergers with other unions, compared to diversification through recruiting new members, mergers represent a more appealing strategy to union leaders. It is cheaper for a union, even a large union in the over-500,000 membership range, to negotiate a merger with a smaller union of 40,000 members than it is to organize eight large industrial plants with 5,000 members each. Moreover, success is more likely in negotiating a merger with a friendly organization than it is in attempting to organize workers in a plant owned by a company hostile to unionization. Hence, it is not surprising that the pace of mergers among American unions, and the concomitant membership diversification, has increased in the past decade. (According to the Bureau of Labor Statistics, over 60 percent of all the mergers in the post-war period have occurred in the past twelve years [U.S. Department of Labor 1980a].)

However in the long run, diversification is a limited strategy. First, as union membership becomes more concentrated in a few large organizations, the possibility for mergers decreases. Second, mergers do not increase the overall membership base of the labor movement. That base is still being eroded. Third, the merger strategy puts unions in competition with each other, using the scarce resources of the labor movement for internal battles. Thus, diversification and merger may be only temporary solutions to organizational decline. Ultimately, unions will have to look toward new sources of power--to both new organizing drives and increased cooperation with non-labor groups.

However, the question remains whether or not labor leaders are responding to the changing economic, social, and political environment fast enough to protect shrinking organizational resources. Unions representing public and service sector workers, e.g. the American Federation of State, County, and Municipal Employees (AFSCME), the Service Employees International Union (SEIU), and the Communication Workers of America (CWA), have been organizing new workers. Large industrial unions, e.g. International Association of Machinists, United Automobile Workers, and the USWA, are only slowly adopting strategies to organize new workers in economic sectors and geographic regions previously underrepresented by unions (*Business Week* 19 Oct. 1981; *Chicago Tribune* 5 Oct. 1981). However, given the weakened resources of unions--in part weakened by a decade-long defensive merger strategy which has added no new resources to the movement--observers are skeptical of unions' ability to make major inroads in new sectors very quickly. There are a number of formidable obstacles to unions attempting to organize in these new areas. These include more sophisticated corporate strategies in keeping out unions (e.g. the increased use of consultants specializing in anti-union campaigns), strong traditional anti-union sentiment in areas such as the South, jurisdictional disputes between unions themselves over who should organize whom, and the need for more innovative strategies on the part of industrial unions not experienced at organizing white-collar workers.

Top union leaders have also appeared reluctant to use innovative strategies in dealing with modern-day threats to unions. For example, in dealing with plant shutdowns and the resulting loss of jobs, most international union officials have worked to ameliorate the negative effects through collective bargaining agreements and negotiations with the corporations, e.g. seeking severance pay, transfer rights to other plants owned by the same company, or early retirement benefits. While these solutions may ease the sting of job loss in the short run, they do not eliminate the negative effects of shutdowns for workers and their communities in the long run. The alternative strategy of joining with other community groups and public interest organizations in questioning corporate decision making, i.e. inter-organizational strategies, has not been widely used.

Thus to summarize, union leaders appear quite reticent to adopt *inter*-organizational strategies for two reasons. First, to union leaders, alliances mean sharing power, which is not an attractive policy to them. Second, compared to labor organizations in many other countries, the American labor movement has a history of isolation from non-labor interest groups. Recently there have been some weak signs that American union leaders may be receptive to inter-organizational linkages as a source of power. Unions have turned to non-labor organizations for support in the early 1980s, as employers' anti-union activities have increased and political support for union-sponsored legislation has decreased--particularly at the Federal level (*Business Week* 5 Oct. 1981). The September 1981 Washington, D.C. "Solidarity Day" demonstration sponsored by the AFL-CIO is another recent sign of labor cooperation with other organizations. However these inter-organizational linkages appear to be more the product of non-labor group initiatives and grassroots union member initiatives than the result of unilateral political activity by top-level labor leaders.

Stopping the Decline: The Membership's Perspective

In seeking a strategy for dealing with pressing issues of the 1980s, e.g. plant closings and deterioration of protective legislation, rank-and-file union members are likely to see more immediate growth in their political power through the establishment of alliances with non-labor interest groups. To rank-and-file organizations, the development of alliances represents a potential means of gaining more power. In contrast, expansion of union membership represents, at best, a long-term potential for an overall increase in union power. This does not mean that grassroots members are likely to oppose organizing drives; it does mean that they are more likely to benefit from organizing activity when it is combined with inter-organizational alliances.

Much of the existing limited cooperation between labor and non-labor groups in the 1970s and 1980s has been forged at local, not national, levels. Local union leaders and unofficial rank-and-file groups have been responsible for labor's presence in public interest organizations such as Illinois Public Action Council, Oregon Fair Share, Massachusetts Fair Share, Connecticut Citizen Action Group, and Pennsylvania Public Interest Coalition (*New York Times* 1 Sept. 1980). Also, one of the major successes of the American anti-nuclear movement--the Bailly Alliance's 1981 victory in stopping construction of the Northern Indiana Public Service Company's nuclear power plant near Gary, Indiana--is a prominent recent example of a locally based political coalition relying on strong support from local labor union activists. Commenting on the local nature of the new alliances, Heather Booth--a community organizer and executive director of the Citizen-Labor Energy Coalition--states that

> Labor is responding to inflation and unemployment by forging new alliances with others bearing the burden of the troubled economy. This stems from labor's traditional social concern. But previously this concern was focused primarily through national lobbying and legislation. Now unions are developing local organizational alliances [*New York Times* 1 Sept. 1980].

Although one reason for local unionist involvement in alliances has been their concern for the overall union movement, another reason has been their immediate concern with how the changing economy has affected their community. The impact of the economic restructuring of the 1970s and 1980s has been disproportionately felt in specific geographical areas and by particular social groups. For example, the economic devastation felt by Youngstown, Ohio residents--who witnessed the loss of over 10,000 jobs due to steel plant shutdowns--sparked the formation of a regional labor-community alliance alliance (Fuechtman 1981; Lynd 1982; Moberg 1979).

Another reason for local union involvement in alliances, has been the disproportionate burden borne by minority workers in the shutdown of plants in core industries. Many of these industries--most notably auto and steel--have provided substantial numbers of Blacks and Hispanics with well-paying stable employment. Five percent of all Black earnings in the United States are made by Blacks employed in the automobile industry.[2] Contraction of the automobile industry is having a devastating effect on the Black community. A recent study of plant shutdowns and plant relocation has shown that Blacks have disproportionately borne the negative effects of plant closure and relocation (Squires 1981). Because of this, civil rights groups are increasingly cooperating with workers affected or threatened by shutdowns when workers seek local, state, and Federal remedies to the crisis. Unlike the rank-and-file workers and local union leaders who have become involved in these alliances, top union leaders have not generally seen such inter-organizational linkages as serving their interests.

POTENTIAL FOR A RENEWED MOVEMENT

What has been a rational response by union leaders to the employment decline in key industrial sectors may not have been a rational response for the worker or for the broader union movement. The scarce resources of American labor organizations are now more scarce. Given continued structural shifts in the economy, including the changing character of the workforce and the changing strategies of business and industry, labor organizations are threatened with membership erosion and a declining influence in the workplace and in society. In terms of its social impact, the present changing economic structure may be analogous to the shift from competitive capitalism to monopoly capitalism which took place in the first decades of this century. Of relevance to the present study is the response of labor organizations to such shifts. In the early twentieth century the lack of any effective response resulted in the deterioration of union organizations. Will the response of contemporary unions be similar? This largely depends on the relative strength of top union leaders in protecting their interests and local union activists' ability in asserting their interests.

The options available to labor appear to be either a slow decline using the top leaderships' intra-organizational survival strategies or stabilization and possibly growth using grassroots-supported intra-organizational *and* inter-organizational survival strategies. With the weakening of the overall union movement, top union leaders' influence is likely to diminish vis-a-vis grassroots members and local leaders.

It should be noted that progressive rank-and-file activity among Canadian USWA members has always been significant and has been growing in recent years. This has been a product of a more progressive tradition of union politics, Canadian nationalism, an expanding Canadian steel industry, and an economic crisis in the broader Canadian economy. Although the role of the Canadian "minority" within the International union has had some impact on USWA politics, a thorough analysis of Canadian Steelworker politics is beyond the scope of the present book. A more detailed account of the role of Canadian members in USWA politics is provided in Nyden (1979:ch. 9).

Emphasis on inter-organizational linkages as a means of increasing organizational strength has major implications for the ideology and organizational structure of the American labor movement. First, it commits labor to a policy of broader involvement in American politics. Second, given the tendency for linkages to occur at the *local* level, where social movement organizations have been stronger, the opportunity for rank-and-file workers and local union leaders to exert more influence over labor organizations previously characterized by centralized leadership is likely to increase.

This does raise another question as to whether or not rank-and-file leaders and their organizations will maintain their links to the grassroots membership if they do gain power. While some existing sociological theories--discussed earlier in this book--argue that a separation of leadership and membership interests is likely to occur, this is not an inevitable outcome given the social process of change described here. Quite the opposite is true. Given the present political and economic environment, any rejuvenated reform movement is likely to be closely linked to local social networks. Rank-and-file movements will derive their support from local unionists and will succeed only insofar as they continue to receive it. The presence or absence of the social links between workers and grassroots leaders--as well as the social factors influencing the strength and character of those links--are of central importance in understanding the past, present, and future of the rank-and-file union movement. The degree to which the movement is able to broaden its base, while maintaining its social ties to the rank and file, will determine the future of the movement and most likely the future of the union movement.

Appendix A

A Methodology

Field studies of political insurgencies within large organizations require methodologies designed to gain a detailed understanding of the roots, structure, and goals of the contending parties. This does not necessarily mean that all factions in the conflict must be studied by the same researcher. In fact, a sociologist who is detached and not closely involved in the activities of any one of the political camps may find his or her efforts less fruitful than those of a researcher intimately involved in the affairs of just *one* camp.

The present fieldwork project involved intensive observation of one of the groups involved in the organizational conflict, rather than observation of all sides in the conflict. The tactic of "taking sides" has been used by sociologists studying social settings experiencing similar types of conflict. In his article, "Participant Observation and the Collection and Interpretation of Data," Arthur Vidich explains that a fieldworker's "neutrality" in a setting of social conflict implies to the parties in the conflict

> a specific attitude toward the issue--being above it, outside it, more important than it, not interested in it. Whatever meanings respondents attach to neutrality will, henceforth, be used as a further basis for response.... Failure to make a commitment can create resentment, hostility, and antagonism just as easily as taking a stand. In both cases, but each in its own way, relationships will be altered and, hence, data will be affected [1969:84].

Vidich adds that

> Consequently it is hardly possible to conform to the standards of an entire society, and hence, to follow a general policy of conformity is to follow no policy at all. Any policy which is designed to guide the field worker's actions must be based on a deliberate judgment as to which sources of information must be used to secure data [ibid.:83].

Since less is typically known and written about insurgents and their organizations than is known about top union officials and the official union organization, I focused my research on *grassroots critics* of the top United Steelworkers of America leadership rather than on the incumbent union leadership itself.

Field research of the rank-and-file movement in the USWA was best completed from a base within the industrial community. Therefore, in September 1975, my wife and I moved to Hammond, Indiana--a city situated in the middle of the Chicago-Northwest Indiana industrial region, which is also the heart of the largest District in the USWA, District 31. We lived in the area for four years. In addition to spending time on the research project, I had a full-time teaching and administrative position at Calumet College--a small private college in Hammond. While there were times when the dual work pressures of teaching and doing research seemed to conflict, the teaching position did provide the financial support necessary both to carry out the research and to provide a roof over my head and food on my table. Because the position at the college involved both teaching and serving as the college's "Community Organization Counselor"--a liaison between the college and various community organizations--I was given greater legitimacy in the community than someone who was just there "temporarily" to do research. By living and working in the community, breathing the same polluted air, and having the same concerns over the same local issues, I was able to gain a better understanding of the broader aspects of the industrial community, i.e. its politics, its lifestyles, and its physical environment.

It also provided me with a greater legitimacy in the eyes of rank-and-file Steelworkers. Three years after moving to the area, I met one of the local rank-and-file activists at a retirement dinner sponsored by one of the local unions (a dinner I was attending as part of my work as Calumet College Community Organization Counselor). He told me that he was "impressed" by my "continued interest" in the union. He indicated that most of the other individuals who had done research on the union practiced "hit-and-run research"; they just visited the community for a few days or a few weeks, collected their interviews, and left, never to be heard from again.

My research was viewed by rank-and-file activists as more of a two-way process. While I was collecting data for "my own purposes"--first for my Ph.D. dissertation and later for this book--I was also responding to their questions about what I was finding. I have spoken to rank-and-file caucuses and met with various rank-and-file activists to discuss both the results of the study and the implications for rank-and-file organizations seeking to bring about change in the union. One caucus has used material I have written as part of an orientation for new members.

In regard to the specific research techniques themselves, I relied primarily on interviews with rank-and-file activists and

participant   observation   of   rank-and-file   organization
activity--at local, regional, and national levels.   Although a
few of the interviews were completed in New York and
Baltimore while I was still attending classes at the University
of Pennsylvania and living in Philadelphia, most of the
interviews were completed after we moved to the Midwest.   The
respondent sample was built through the "snowballing" of
contacts--asking each interviewee for names of other activists
to whom I should talk.   Initial key contacts were established
with rank-and-file leaders who were prominent in USWA
Convention debates or who were mentioned in local media
reports.   Contacts outside of the Chicago area were identified
using both my existing Chicago contacts and media sources.
In the course of soliciting the more than 120 interviews used
in this dissertation, only two persons refused to speak with
me.

Interviews were usually taped, unless the interviewee
requested that they not be recorded.   The average interview
lasted two to three hours and took place in the individual's
home.   Interviews consisted of open-ended questions on
general topics identified early in my research.   They were
unstructured insofar as I would ask questions in response to a
point made by the interviewee--questions I had not necessarily
intended to ask at the beginning of the interview.   The
flexibility of this research method proved useful in exploring
the nature of rank-and-file politics--an area that has received
little research attention in the past and an area about which
few previous research findings exist as substantive guides for
surveys and interviews.   It was also a research method that
was sensitive to the changing and complex nature of
rank-and-file politics.   It provided me with a way of
"discovering" social phenomena that might have escaped the
eyes of a sociologist using more structured interviews or
surveys.   In essence my method of collecting data, analyzing
it, and identifying implications for existing sociological theory
incorporated the model described in Barney G. Glaser and
Anselm L. Strauss's The Discovery of Grounded Theory
(1967).   In this methodology one attempts to minimize the
number of preconceived notions one has before entering the
field; rather, in the process of completing the research one
develops hypotheses and their implications for theory.

In addition to interviewing activists, I attended numerous
local union rank-and-file caucus meetings, local union
meetings, rallies, fund-raising events, national insurgent
organization campaign events, and USWA International
Conventions.   Campaign activities, including rallies, leafleting,
and office work, were also observed.   In some of these
activities I was more of a participant observer than I was an
observer (it is rather difficult for a researcher to justify his
presence in front of a factory gate at 5:30 in the morning by
saying he is "just watching" others hand out campaign

material).   During all of these activities I was talking with rank-and-file activists, developing insights into the research issues and developing new contacts.   This direct personal involvement in rank-and-file activities, combined with the open-ended unstructured interviews, provided sociological data unobtainable through other research methodologies.

Appendix B

Tables and Figures

Steel Furnace Capacity, 1936 - 1960
(millions of tons)

Year	Capacity	Year	Capacity
1936	78.2	1950	100.1
1937	78.1	1951	104.2
1938	80.2	1952	108.6
1939	81.8	1953	117.5
		1954	124.3
1940	81.6		
1941	85.2	1955	125.8
1942	88.9	1956	128.4
1943	90.6	1957	133.5
1944	93.9	1958	140.7
		1959	147.6
1945	95.5		
1946	91.9	1960	148.6
1947	91.2		
1948	94.2		
1949	96.1		

SOURCE: American Iron and Steel Institute 1961.

Table 3.2

Steel Industry Profits, 1935 - 1981
(After-tax income as Percentage of Total Revenue)

Year	Profit Rate	Year	Profit Rate
1935	3.0	1960	5.7
1936	6.3	1961	5.2
1937	7.7	1962	4.1
1938	-0.9*	1963	5.4
1939	5.2	1964	6.1
1940	8.0	1965	5.9
1941	6.0	1966	5.9
1942	3.4	1967	4.9
1943	2.8	1968	5.3
1944	2.7	1969	4.6
1945	3.1	1970	2.8
1946	5.5	1971	2.8
1947	6.1	1972	3.4
1948	6.7	1973	4.4
1949	7.1	1974	6.5
1950	8.0	1975	4.7
1951	5.8	1976	3.7
1952	5.0	1977	0.1
1953	5.6	1978	2.8
1954	6.0	1979	2.1
1955	7.8	1980	3.0
1956	7.3	1981	4.2
1957	7.3		
1958	6.3		
1959	5.8		

*Loss.

SOURCES: American Iron and Steel Institute 1960 (for data from 1935-53), 1982 (for data from 1979-81); and U.S. Congress 1980 (for data from 1954-78).

Table 4.1

Imports as a Percentage of Apparent U.S. Steel Supply

Year*	Percentage	Year	Percentage
1950-55	1.8	1975	13.5
1956-60	3.3	1976	14.1
		1977	17.8
1961	4.7	1978	18.1
1962	5.6	1979	15.2
1963	6.9		
1964	7.3	1980	16.3
		1981	19.1
1965	10.3		
1966	10.9		
1967	12.2		
1968	16.7		
1969	13.7		
1970	13.8		
1971	17.0		
1972	16.6		
1973	12.4		
1974	13.4		

*Figures for 1950-55 and 1956-60 are averages for those periods.

SOURCE: American Iron and Steel Institute 1971, 1980, 1981, 1982.

Table 4.2

Comparison of Japanese and U.S. Costs of Finished Steel
Ratio of Japanese to American Costs
(Cost in dollars per net ton)

Year	Basic Cost	Total Material Cost	Basic Labor Cost
1956	1.08	1.66	.49
1957	1.21	2.14	.44
1958	.81	1.32	.43
1959	.79	1.37	.38
1960	.71	1.28	.32
1961	.75	1.39	.30
1962	.69	1.21	.34
1963	.68	1.19	.34
1964	.65	1.13	.31
1965	.68	1.13	.34
1966	.63	1.08	.31
1967	.59	1.04	.28
1968	.57	0.96	.30
1969	.56	0.97	.27
1970	.57	0.97	.29
1971	.56	0.87	.33
1972	.54	0.79	.36
1973	.63	0.89	.40
1974	.69	0.91	.42
1975	.59	0.80	.38
1976	.55	0.74	.34

SOURCE: Calculations based on data from Crandall 1981, Table 3-1, 48.

Table 4.3

Capital Expenditures on Productive Steelmaking Facilities*
(millions of 1978 dollars)

Year	Expenditure	Year	Expenditure
1950	$1,181	1970	$2,214
1952	2,749	1971	1,705
1954	1,258	1972	1,265
1956	2,484	1973	1,630
1958	2,045	1974	2,163
1960	2,675	1975	2,684
1961	1,698	1976	2,599
1962	1,600	1977	2,054
1963	1,811	1978	1,706
1964	2,760		
1965	3,107		
1966	3,405		
1967	3,367		
1968	3,576		
1969	2,869		

*Capital expenditures less environmental expenditures and estimated nonsteel capital expenditures. Current dollars (adjusted by using the GCP Nonresidential Investment Implicit Price Deflator). Capital expenditures shown are for American Iron and Steel Institute reporting companies only.

SOURCE: U.S. Congress 1980, Table 25, p. 123.

Table 4.4

Production of Steel By Furnace Type
(Percent of Total Production)

Year	Basic Oxygen	Electric	Open Hearth
1956	0.4	7.5	92.1
1958	1.6	7.8	90.6
1960	3.4	8.4	88.2
1962	5.7	9.1	85.2
1964	12.2	9.9	77.9
1966	25.3	11.1	63.6
1968	37.1	12.8	50.1
1970	48.2	15.3	36.5
1972	56.0	17.8	26.2
1974	56.0	19.7	24.3
1976	62.5	19.2	18.3
1978	60.9	23.5	15.6
1980	60.4	27.9	11.7
1981	60.6	28.3	11.1

SOURCE: American Iron and Steel Institute 1981, 1982; and Hiestan 1974, p. 15.

Table 4.5

Percent of U.S. Raw Steel Production Continuously Cast

Year	Percent
1969	2.9
1975	9.1
1976	10.6
1977	12.5
1978	15.2
1979	16.9
1980	20.3
1981	21.6

SOURCE: U.S. Congress 1980, p. 289. (for 1969 statistic); and American Iron and Steel Institute 1982 (for all other statistics).

Table 4.6

BLS Index of Output Per Man-Hour in the Steel Industry
(All Employees)

Year	Index (1977=100)	Year	Index
1951	68.1	1970	87.6
1952	68.5	1971	91.9
1953	70.0	1972	97.3
1954	66.8	1973	106.6
		1974	106.5
1955	75.9		
1956	74.8	1975	93.3
1957	72.9	1976	99.0
1958	67.4	1977	100.0
1959	75.7	1978	108.3
		1979	106.9
1960	71.2		
1961	73.4	1980	102.9
1962	77.1	1981	112.0
1963	80.6		
1964	84.1		
1965	87.5		
1966	89.2		
1967	86.4		
1968	89.5		
1969	90.0		

SOURCE: American Iron and Steel Institute 1982.

Table 5.1

Proportion of USWA Membership By Industry, 1969 and 1980

Industry	1969	1980
MANUFACTURING		
Furniture	1.1	1.2
Chemicals	*	3.2
Stone	1.1	2.1
Primary Metals	52.4	40.9
Fabricated Metals	14.4	13.3
Machinery	11.5	11.4
Electrical	1.8	2.3
Transportation	3.5	6.0
NONMANUFACTURING		
Mining	8.1	8.2
Transportation	*	1.0
Electrical	*	1.1
Wholesale/Retail Trade	1.1	1.7
Service	*	1.0
TOTAL MEMBERSHIP	100.0	100.0
	(1,225,087)	(1,238,000)

*=less than 1.0 percent.

SOURCE: Unpublished data provided by the United Steelworkers of America (for 1969) and the U.S. Department of Labor (for 1980).

Table 5.2

Reasons for Initial Caucus and Union Involvement

(Reasons Given by Local 1010 Rank and File Caucus Activists
for Their Initial Involvement in the Caucus and Union)

Reasons Given for Involvement	Number of Respondents*	Percent
Personal contact with a union activist on the job	13	62
Member of family active in the union (not necessarily this one)	5	24
Discrimination	5	24
Through involvement in politics outside the union	3	14
Specific grievance (not discrimination)	3	14
Involved in early organizing drive	2	10

*The total number of respondents is 21. The numbers add up to
than 21 because some respondents have more than one answer.

Table 6.1

Vote Totals for 1977 USWA Presidential Election
(By District)

District	McBride Vote	Sadlowski Vote	Total Vote	Percentage Sadlowski
1	11,212	9,783	20,995	46.6
3	8,423	3,792	12,215	31.0
4	9,789	9,357	19,146	48.9
5	24,655	2,769	27,424	10.1
6	26,434	15,819	42,253	37.4
7	15,331	12,934	28,265	45.8
8	4,773	6,236	11,009	56.6
9	11,717	11,758	23,475	50.1
15	16,101	15,072	31,173	48.3
19	7,716	8,870	16,586	53.5
20	15,702	16,140	31,842	50.7
23	12,606	8,539	21,145	40.4
26	9,516	13,471	22,987	58.6
27	8,992	5,223	14,215	36.7
28	7,005	7,857	14,862	52.9
29	6,287	9,468	15,755	60.1
30	11,479	4,696	16,175	29.0
31	21,932	34,658	56,590	61.2
32	7,161	7,583	14,744	51.4
33	6,698	9,328	16,026	58.2
34	10,581	5,803	16,384	35.4
35	14,260	4,230	18,490	22.9
36	20,834	5,993	26,827	22.3
37	16,865	3,464	20,329	17.0
38	22,792	16,438	39,230	41.9
Total	328,861	249,281	578,142	43.1

SOURCE: United Steelworkers of America 1977a.

Figure 1.1

Social Forces Influencing Union Leadership

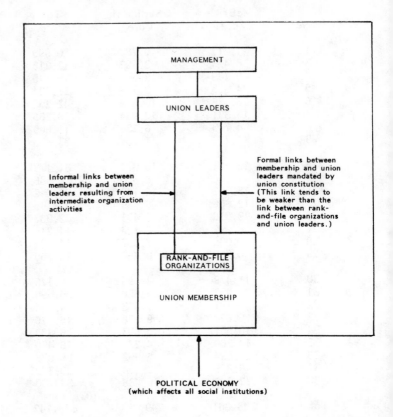

Figure 3.1

Real Wages of Workers in Basic Steel and All Manufacturing
1932 - 1981
(1967 dollars)

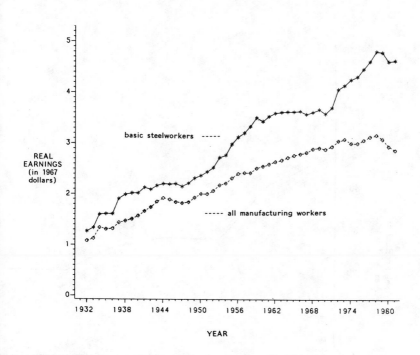

YEAR

SOURCE: Calculations based on data from U.S. Department of Labor
1979, 1980b, 1981, 1982, 1983.

Figure 4.1

U.S. and World Raw Steel Production
(U.S. Production as a Percentage of World Production)

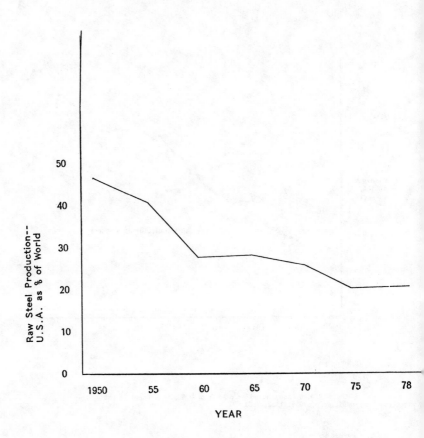

SOURCE: American Iron and Steel Institute 1980, Table II-1, p. 8.

Figure 4.2

Production Workers in the Basic Steel Industry, 1939-1981*
(moving average)**

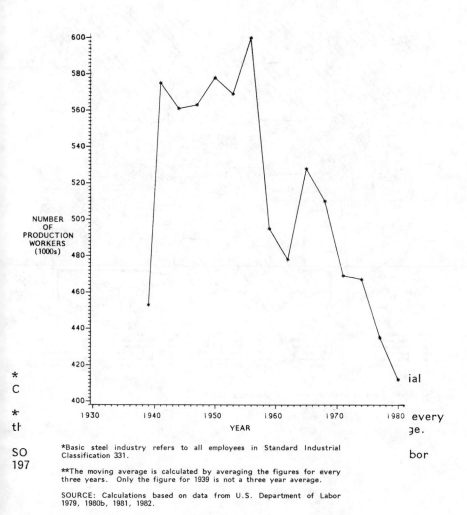

*
C

*·
th

SO
197

ial

every
ge.

bor

*Basic steel industry refers to all employees in Standard Industrial
Classification 331.

**The moving average is calculated by averaging the figures for every
three years. Only the figure for 1939 is not a three year average.

SOURCE: Calculations based on data from U.S. Department of Labor
1979, 1980b, 1981, 1982.

Figure 6.1

1977 USWA International Election Results, by Region

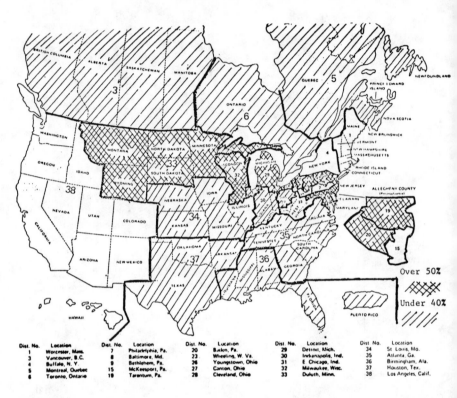

SOURCE: United Steelworkers of America 1977b.

NOTES

CHAPTER 1

[1] This argument is well established and has been presented by a large number of authors: Aronowitz (1973), Braverman (1974), Burawoy (1979), Edwards (1979), Friedman (1977), Herding (1972), Hill (1981), Hyman (1975), R. Pfeffer (1979), and Stone (1975).

[2] A pluralist definition of democracy is given by the authors of a cross-national study of union democracy:

> Democracy in a large organisation or a society is a decision-making system in which the membership actively participates, directly and indirectly through its representatives, in the making and implementation of policy and in the selection of officials, for all levels, on the basis of political equality and majority rule. Furthermore, the system operates on the basis of the accountability of officials, the legitimacy of opposition, and a due process for the protection of the rights of individuals and minorities [Edelstein & Warner, 1975:30].

CHAPTER 2

[1] The radicalization of the political climate during the Great Depression is well documented. Among the more prominent histories are Bernstein (1971), Boyer and Morais (1970), Brecher (1972), and Piven and Cloward (1971).

[2] Computed from figures given by Hogan (1971:3:1181).

[3] This finding is echoed in an account given by John Sargent, who recalls that

> as a result of enthusiasm of the people in the mill you had a series of strikes, wildcats, shutdowns, anything working people could think of to secure for themselves what they decided they had to have. If their wages were low, there was no contract to prohibit them from striking and they struck for better wages. If their conditions were bad, if they didn't like what was going on, if they were being abused, the people in the mills themselves... would

shut down a department or even a group of departments to secure for themselves the things they found necessary [Lynd & Lynd 1973:107-8].

[4] Stone points out that the union

worked with the employers to streamline the old hierarchical system through a mammoth effort to re-evaluate and re-classify 50,000 job titles. The result was that they pegged every job to one of 30 job classifications, which they put in a strict order [with set wage differentials] [ibid.].

CHAPTER 3

[1] U.S. Congress (1980:119-20). Here, the OTA study is using after-tax profit as a percentage of stockholder equity as a unit of comparison.

[2] Much of the information on the Dues Protest Committee is based on a number of interviews with Steelworkers active in DPC in the 1950s. The interviewees included John Askins, John Barbero, William Litch, Alice Peurala, Curtis Strong, and Anthony Tomko.

[3] Under the USWA *Constitution*, a special convention must be held if 25 percent of the locals pass supporting resolutions. The DPC only succeeded in getting 100 of the 700 necessary local union endorsements. However, the post-Convention resolution campaign provided the DPC with the unionwide local contacts needed to underwrite a 1956-57 campaign for the top three International offices (Herling 1972:48-49).

CHAPTER 4

[1] Information on diversification in the 1960s is from Hogan (1971:4:1647-1843).

[2] After incumbent USWA International President McDonald's defeat in 1965, the HRC itself was abandoned, but new negotiating structures maintained the centralized bargaining control forged in 1959 (Betheil 1978:12-20).

CHAPTER 5

[1] The "pro-corporate environment" is specifically discussed in Bluestone and Harrison (1980). Present-day conservative political practices, as exemplified by the right-to-work laws in southern states, combine with past anti-union traditions to create an environment not hospitable to

union activity, much less rank-and-file insurgency. Analyses
of the social history of anti-unionism in the South are given in
Marshall (1968:chs. 1, 18-22), Foner (1974:39, 86-87, 116-19,
337-38, et passim), and *Southern Exposure* (1976).

[2] On the surface this argument may appear to conflict
with the Kerr and Siegel worker-militancy theory, which
argues that isolated, single-industry towns produce more
worker militancy (Kerr & Siegel 1954). However, Southern
communities with mini-mills are not necessarily
isolated--particularly from the pressures of county and state
governments. Moreover, these are communities in which
industry has been introduced quite recently. Often the new
industry provides jobs and creates prosperity that had not
previously existed in such towns. In such a context, worker
militancy appears threatening. Also, given the recent
development of mini-mills, there is no past history of worker
militancy such as there is in most isolated coal-mining
towns--the archtypical worker:community militancy hothouse
described by Kerr and Siegel.

[3] This is also supported by my own observations.

[4] This was the case with a number of steelworkers who
were interviewed: Anonymous, Barbero, Berlin, Haaf, Tomko,
and R. Wood.

CHAPTER 6

[1] The analysis in this section is based on my personal
observations of the campaign organization and its activities, as
well as on my interviews and conversations with numerous
persons involved in the campaign.

[2] An interview with Sadlowski appeared in the January
1977 issue of *Penthouse*. Articles from other sources have
been quoted elsewhere in this chapter.

[3] Even if Sadlowski did win, he would have needed the
backing of much of the International Executive Board if union
reforms were to be enacted and enforced. In the event that
Sadlowski lost and Fight Back District Directors won, the
national organization would have been strengthened by having
spokespersons and supporters at the International level. The
lack of any such strong support was a key factor in the
decline of the rank-and-file movement in the late 1970s and
early 1980s.

[4] Many other rank-and-file Steelworkers agreed with
Montgomery (DeJesus, Julian, B. Morris, and Rospierski).

[5] Another Chicago area union official who supported Sadlowski commented that Sadlowski's "idea is that you go after these offices, you win the office, and *then* you're able to affect policy." He added, "In my gut that particular philosophy has never rung true. Frankly, I've seen nobody with that philosophy get to that position where they can do some good. They've finally copped out and worked for 'the Establishment'" (Anonymous--Hammond).

[6] Data in this section are based on USWA contract data and United Steelworkers of America (1977a). Because local size may have changed between June 1976 and February 1977, e.g. because of plant shutdowns or expansions, there may be some inaccuracies in the application of the contract data to the election results. However, in a 1.2-million-member union with over 5,000 locals, such fluctuations would not significantly affect the data. In addition, sections of the 1977 *Report* are difficult to read because handwritten numbers are illegible. Consequently, there may be a slight variation in the numbers used here. However, the total possible error due to these illegible numbers is less than 200, and hence is relatively insignificant.

CHAPTER 8

[1] The idea that the news is something that is "produced" by the media is nothing new. One of the more recent examples of such an analysis is Gans (1980).

[2] Bill Moyers, narrative in *The Detroit Model* (film), Al Levin and WNET producers, Media at Work/California Newsreel, distributors, 1980.

BIBLIOGRAPHY

Abel, I.W. 1976. *Collective Bargaining, Labor Relations in Steel: Then and Now.* New York: Columbia University Press.

American Iron and Steel Institute. 1960. *Annual Statistical Report, 1959.* Washington, D.C.: AISI.

1961 *Annual Statistical Report, 1960.* Washington, D.C.: AISI.

1971 *Annual Statistical Report, 1970.* Washington, D.C.: AISI.

1980 *Steel at the Crossroads.* Washington, D.C.: AISI.

1981 *Annual Statistical Report, 1980.* Washington, D.C.: AISI.

1982 *Annual Statistical Report, 1981.* Washington, D.C.: AISI.

Aronowitz, Stanley. 1973. *False Promises.* New York: McGraw-Hill.

Averitt, Robert T. 1968. *The Dual Economy: The Dynamics of American Industrial Structure.* New York: Norton.

Barks, Joseph V. 1980. "In the Land of Cotton, the Profit's Now in Steel." *Iron Age*, 3 March, 26-30.

Benson, Kenneth. 1977. "Innovation and Crisis in Organizational Analysis." *Sociological Quarterly*, 18:3-16.

Bernstein, Irving. 1971. *The Turbulent Years.* Boston: Houghton Mifflin.

Betheil, Richard. 1978. "The ENA in Perspective: The Transformation of Collective Bargaining in the Basic Steel Industry." *Review of Radical Political Economics*, 10 (Summer):1-24.

Bluestone, Barry and Bennett Harrison. 1980. *Capital and Communities: The Causes and Consequences of Private Disinvestment.* Washington, D.C.: Progressive Alliance.

Blumer, Herbert. 1955. "Collective Behavior." In *Principles of Sociology*, ed. Alfred McClung Lee. New York: Barnes & Noble, pp. 165-222.

Boyer, Richard O., and Herbert Morais. 1970. *Labor's Untold Story.* New York: United Electrical, Radio & Machine Workers of America.

Braverman, Harry. 1974. *Labor and Monopoly Capital.* New York: Monthly Review Press.

Brecher, Jeremy. 1972. *Strike.* Greenwich, Conn.: Fawcett.

Brody, David. 1969. *Steelworkers in America: The Nonunion Era.* New York: Harper Torchbooks.

Brody, M. 1981. "Strength in Steel." *Barrons*, 5 Oct.

Burawoy, Michael. 1979. *Manufacturing Consent*: *Changes in the Labor Process under Monopoly Capitalism.* Chicago: University of Chicago Press.

Business Week. "A try at steel-mill harmony," 29 June, p. 132+; 5 Oct.; "Steel Jacks Up Its Productivity," 12 Oct., p. 84+; 19 Oct.; "Is Big Steel Abandoning Steel?" 7 Dec. 1981, pp. 34-35; "A Steel Mill that Only Workers Can Rescue," 15 March, p. 27; "U.S. Steelmakers Slim Down for Survival," 31 May, pp. 88=89; "Steel Sees No Exit from Its Depression," 9 Aug. 1982, pp. 24-25; "Steel's Big Labor Savings Are Still Ahead," 14 March 1983, p. 29+.

Chicago Tribune. 1981. "Fortunes Shaky for Labor Unions," 5 Oct, Sect. IV, p. 14.

Cole, Robert E. 1980. *Work, Mobility and Participation*: *A Comparative Study of American and Japanese Industry.* Berkeley: University of California Press.

Compass (Hammond, Indiana). 1976. 5 April.

Conroy, John. 1977. "Mill Town," fourth of a series. *Chicago*, 26 (Feb.):106-15+.

Crandall, Robert W. 1981. *Steel Industry in Recurrent Crisis*: *Policy Options in a Competitive World.* Washington, D.C.: Brookings Institution.

Edelstein, David, and Malcolm Warner. 1975. *Comparative Union Democracy.* London: George Allen & Unwin.

Edwards, Richard. 1979. *Contested Terrain*: *The Transformation of the Workplace in the Twentieth Century.* New York: Basic Books.

Fireman, Bruce, and William A. Gamson. 1979. "Utilitarian Logic in the Resource Mobilization Perspective." In Zald and McCarthy (1979:8-44).

Foner, Philip S. 1974. *Organized Labor and the Black Worker, 1619-1973.* New York: Praeger.

Fortune. 1957. "Revolt in Steel," 55 (Feb.):205.

Foster, William Z. 1971. *The Great Steel Strike and Its Lessons.* New York: DeCapo.

Friedman, Andrew L. 1977. *Industry and Labour*: *Class Struggle at Work and Monopoly Capitalism.* London: Macmillan Press.

Fuechtman, Thomas G. 1981. *Steeples and Stacks*: *A Case Study of the Youngstown Ecumenical Coalitions.* Ph.D. dissertation, University of Chicago, Chicago.

Gans, Herbert J. 1980. *Deciding What's News.* New York: Vintage.

Garner, Roberta Ash. 1977. *Social Movements in America*, 2nd ed. Chicago: Rand McNally.

Glaser, Barney G., and Anselm L. Strauss. 1967. *The Discovery of Grounded Theory*: *Strategies for Qualitative Research.* New York: Aldine.

Goldman, Paul, and Donald R. VanHouten. 1977. "Managerial Strategies and the Worker: A Marxist Analysis of Bureaucracy." *Sociological Quarterly*, 18:108-25.

Harbison, Frederick. 1938. *Collective Bargaining in the Steel Industry*. Princeton, N.J.: Princeton University Press.

Hardman, J.B.S. 1972. *Labor at the Rubicon*. New York: New York University Press.

Herding, Richard. 1972. *Job Control and Union Structure*. Rotterdam, Netherlands: Rotterdam University Press.

Herling, John. 1972. *Right to Challenge*. New York: Harper & Row.

Heydebrand, Wolf. 1977. "Organizational Contradictions in Public Bureaucracies: Toward a Marxian Theory of Organizations." *Sociological Quarterly*, 18:83-107.

Hiestand, Dale L. 1974. *High Level Manpower and Technological Change in the Steel Industry*. New York: Praeger.

Hill, Stephen. 1981. *Competition and Control of Work*: *The New Industrial Sociology*. Cambridge, Mass.: MIT Press.

Hogan, William T. 1971. *Economic History of the Iron and Steel Industry in the United States*, 5 vols. Lexington, Mass.: Lexington Books.

Hyman, Richard. 1975. *Industrial Relations*: *A Marxist Introduction*. London: Macmillan.

Hyman, Richard, and R. H. Fryer, eds. 1977. *Trade Unions under Capitalism*. Glasgow: Fontana.

Ignatius, David. 1977. "The Press in Love." *Columbia Journalism Review*, 16:26-27.

In These Times. "Union Wins Modest Gains in Steel Talks," 23-29 April 1980; "Some Steel Insurgents Blame Selves for Losses," 17-30 June 1981.

Interchurch World Movement. 1920. *Report on the Steel Strike of 1919*. New York: Harcourt, Brace & Howe.

Iron Age. "'Margins Are Going to Have to Improve,' National's Love," 4 May 1981, pp. 37-41.

Kelly, Edward, and Mark Shutes. 1979. "Lykes: A Case Study of a Shaky Conglomerate." *Business & Society Review*, 28:38-41.

Kerr, Clark, and Abraham Siegel. 1954. "The Inter-industry Propensity to Strike: An International Comparison." In *Industrial Conflict*, ed. A. Kornhauser et al. New York: McGraw-Hill, pp. 189-212.

Kirkland, Richard L., Jr. 1981a. "Big Steel Recasts Itself." *Fortune*, 103 (6 April):28-34.

   1981b "Pilgrams' Profits at Nucor." *Fortune*, 103 (6 April):43-44+.

Kornblum, William. 1974. *Blue Collar Community*. Chicago: University of Chicago Press.

Kotz, Nick. 1976. "Oil Can Eddie Takes on the Old Guard." *New York Times Magazine*, 19 Dec., pp. 32-33+.

Lester, Richard. 1958. *As Unions Mature*. Princeton, N.J.: Princeton University Press.

Lipset, Seymour Martin, Martin Trow, and James Coleman. 1956. *Union Democracy*. Garden City, N.Y.: Anchor.

Local 1010 Steelworker. 1981. "Jack Parton Speaks: An Interview with the Director," 19 Nov., p. 12.

Los Angeles Times. 14 Sept. 1976.

Lynd, Alice, and Staughton Lynd. 1973. *Rank and File*: *Personal Histories by Working Class Organizers*. Boston: Beacon.

Lynd, Staughton. 1982. *The Fight Against Shutdowns*: *Youngstown's Steel Mill Closings*. San Pedro: Singlejack Books.

McCarthy, John D. and Mayer N. Zald. 1977. "Resource Mobilization and Social Movements: A Partial Theory." *American Journal of Sociology*, 82:1212-41.

McManus, George J. 1979. "Just How Close Is the Push-Button Steel Mill?" *Iron Age*, 1 Oct., pp. MP3-11.

   1980a "Minimills Begin to Make Noises in a Big Way." *Iron Age*, 5 May, pp. MP5-15.

   1980b "Steel's Headaches Won't Go Away in the Morning." *Iron Age*, 12 May, pp. 27-34.

   1981 "We Are What We Are: Bethlehem's Trautlein." *Iron Age*, 14 April, pp. 43-47.

Marshall, F. Ray. 1967. *Labor in the South*. Cambridge, Mass.: Harvard University Press.

Michels, Robert. 1962. *Political Parties*. New York: Free Press.

Moberg, David. 1979. *Shutdown*. Washington, D.C.: Institute for Policy Studies.

Molotch, Harvey. 1979. "Media and Movements." In Zald and McCarthy (1979:71-93).

Moyers, Bill. 1980. Narrative in *The Detroit Model* (film), Al Levin and WNET, producers, Media at Work/California Newsreel, distributers.

New York Times. "Insurgent Steel Union Campaign Begun with Attack on Abel, Meany," 14 Sept. 1976, p. 22; "Labor's Alliances" (op ed column by Heather Booth), 1 Sept. 1980, p. A13; "Quality Circles Aid Productivity," 25 May, p. D1+; "The Rise of Mini-Steel Mills," 23 Sept., p. D1+; "U.S. Plans Direct Complaints to Nations Subsidizing Steel," 6 Nov., p. 1+ (National edition); "Steel: To Diversify or Rebuild?" 23 Nov. 1981, p. D1+; "The Shrinking Steel Industry," 24 Jan., p. 21+ (National edition); and "Steel Union Leaders Ratify Concessions," 2 March 1983, p. 10 (National edition) (Citations are for New York edition unless otherwise noted.)

Newsweek. "Oil-Can Eddie," 10 May 1976, p. 90+.

Nyden, Philip W. 1976. "Sadlowski and the New Insurgency." *Nation*, 223 (18 Sept.):241-44.

   1979 *Rank-and-File Insurgency in a Large Industrial Union*: *A Case Study of the United Steelworkers of America*. Ph.D. dissertation, University of Pennsylvania, Philadelphia.

   1983 "Evolution of Black Political Influence in American Trade Unions." *Journal of Black Studies*, June.

Oberschall, Anthony.   1973.   *Social Conflict and Social Movements.*   Englewood Cliffs, N.J.: Prentice-Hall.

Olson, Mancur, Jr.   1963.   "Rapid Economic Growth as a Destabilizing Force."   *Journal of Economic History,* 23:529-52.

1968   *Logic of Collective Action.*   New York: Schocken.

Parker, Mike, and Dwight Hansen.   1983.   "The Circle Game." *The Progressive.*   47 (Jan.):32-35.

Pfeffer, Jeffrey.   1978.   *Organizational Design.*   Arlington Heights, Ill.: AHM Publishing.

Pfeffer, Richard M.   1979.   *Working for Capitalism.*   New York: Columbia University Press.

Piven, Frances Fox, and Richard A. Cloward.   1971. *Regulating the Poor.*   New York: Pantheon.

Ramparts.   Dec. 1972.

Rusticus.   1977.   "The Sadlowski Campaign."   *Radical America,* 11 (Jan.-Feb.):75-78.

Sadlowski for District 31 Director.   1973a.   Untitled campaign leaflet.

1973b   "Sadlowski Says It's Ours to Change (campaign leaflet).

1974   "Its Ours to Change" (campaign leaflet).

Scaff, Lawrence A.   1981.   "Max Weber and Robert Michels." *American Journal of Sociology,* 86:1269-86.

Serrin, William.   1974.   *The Company and the Union.*   New York: Vintage.

Southern Exposure.   1976.   Special issue on Southern labor, 4 (Spring/Summer).

Squires, Gregory D.   1981.   "'Runaway Plants,' Capital Mobility and Black Economic Rights: The Limitations of Affirmative Action as a Strategy for Black Liberation." Paper presented at the Conference on New Perspectives on the Urban Political Economy, 22-24, May Washington, D.C.

Steelworkers Fight Back.   1976, 1977.   Campaign literature.

Stone, Katherine.   1975.   "The Origins of Job Structures in the Steel Industry."   In *Root & Branch: The Rise of the Workers' Movements,* ed. Root & Branch. Greenwich, Conn.: Fawcett Crest, 1975, pp. 123-57.

Ulman, Lloyd.   1962.   *The Government of the Steel Worker's Union.*   New York: John Wiley.

U.S. Congress.   1980.   Office of Technological Assessment. *Technology and Steel Industry Competitiveness.* Washington, D.C.: Supt. of Documents.

U.S. Department of Labor.   1975.   Bureau of Labor Statistics. *Technological Change in Manpower Trends in Five Industries: Pulp and Paper/Hydraulic Cement/Steel/Aircraft and Missiles/Wholesale Trade.* Bulletin 1856.

1979   *Employment and Earnings, United States, 1909-78.* Bulletin 1312-11.

1980a   *Directory of National Union and Employee Associations, 1979.*   Bulletin 2079.

1980b *Supplement to Employment and Earnings: Revised Establishment Data.* September 1980.
1981 *Employment and Earnings,* 28 (March).
1982 *Employment and Earnings,* 29 (March).
1983 *Monthly Labor Review,* 106 (Jan.).
U.S. General Accounting Office. 1981. *Report to the Congress of the United States: New Strategy Required for Aiding Distressed Steel Industry.* Washington, D.C.: U.S. Supt. of Documents.
United Steelworkers of America. 1950. *Proceedings of the Fifth Constitutional Convention, 1950.* Pittsburgh, Pa.: USWA.
1968 *Proceedings of the 14th Constitutional Convention, 1968.* Pittsburgh, Pa.: USWA.
1974 *Then and Now: The Road Between.* Pittsburgh, Pa.: USWA.
1977a *Report on the International Election, April 28, 1977.* Pittsburgh, Pa.: USWA.
1977b The Union (pamphlet). Pittsburgh, Pa.: USWA.
1982 *Constitution.* Adopted at the 21st Constitutional Convention.
United Steelworkers of America, District 31. Files.
Vidich, Arthur J. 1969. "Participant Observation and the Collection and Interpretation of Data." In *Issues in Participant Observation,* ed. George J. McCall and J.L. Simmons. Reading, Mass.:Addison-Wesley, pp. 78-87.
Village Voice. 1975 20 Oct.
Wall Street Journal. "Steel Firms' Suprising 3rd Quarter Results Put Analysts in Mood to Rework Bearish Estimates," 2 Nov. 1981, p. 55; "USW Ratifies Contract with Pay Cuts and Company Promises to Invest in Steel," 2 March 1983. p. 2.
Washington Post. 23 March 1975, pp B1-B2.
Weber, Arnold R. 1980. "The Steel Labor Agreement: A Better Deal for Industry Than It Appears." *Dun's Review,* 116 (July):10.
Weber, Max. 1958a. "Bureaucracy." In *From Max Weber: Essays in Sociology,* trans. and ed. H.H. Gerth and C. Wright Mills. New York: Oxford University Press, pp. 196-244.
1958b "Politics as a Vocation." In ibid., pp. 77-128.
Wright, Erik Olin. 1974. "To Control or Smash Bureaucracy: Weber and Lenin on Politics, the State, and Bureaucracy." *Berkeley Journal of Sociology,* 19:69-108.
Youngstown Vindicator. 30 Oct. 1976.

Zald, Mayer N., and John D. McCarthy, eds. 1979. *The Dynamics of Social Movements: Resource Mobilization, Social Control, and Tactics.* Cambridge, Mass.: Winthrop.

INTERVIEWS

Amos, Bill. Conversation, East Chicago, Indiana, 29 Sept. 1976.
Anonymous. Conversation, Gary, Indiana, 1981.
Anonymous. Interview, Chicago, Illinois, 1976.
Anonymous. Interview, Gary, Indiana, 1976.
Anonymous. Interview, Hammond, Indiana, 1976.
Anonymous. Interview, Hammond, Indiana, 1976.
Anonymous. Interview, Chicago, Illinois, 1977.
Anonymous. Interview, Hammond, Indiana, 1977.
Anonymous. Interview, Pittsburgh, Pennsylvania, 1977.
Arsenault, Larry. Interview, Toronto, Ontario, 22 Nov. 1976.
Askins, John. Interviews, Chicago, Illinois, 6 Nov. 1975; 22 June 1977.
Backus, Mike. Interview, Madison, Illinois, 30 Dec. 1976.
Bains, Jim. Interview, Birmingham, Alabama, 21 Dec. 1976.
Balanoff, Clem. Interview, Chicago, Illinois, 6 Nov. 1975.
Balanoff, Jim. Interview, Hammond, Indiana, 27 May 1976; conversations, 1976-1983.
Barbero, John. Interviews, Niles, Ohio, 31 July and 31 Oct. 1976.
Berlin, Jim. Interview, Buffalo, New York, 16 Aug. 1976; conversations, Las Vegas, Nevada, 30 Aug.-3 Sept. 1976.
Black, Bob. Conversation, Toronto, Ontario, 22 Nov. 1976.
Booker, Henry. Interview, Birmingham, Alabama, 21 Dec. 1976.
Britton, Louis. Interview, Gary, Indiana, 5 June 1976.
Danzey, C.L. Interview, Birmingham, Alabama, 21 Dec. 1976.
Davis, Fred. Interview, Bridgeport, Connecticut, 6 Aug. 1976.
Davis, Jim. Interview, Girard, Ohio, 31 July 1976; conversation, Chicago, Illinois, 25 Oct. 1976.
DeJesus, Al ("Freddie"). Interview, East Chicago, Indiana, 31 March, 1976.
DelVecchio, John. Interview, Bridgeport, Connecticut, 6 Aug. 1976.
Dennis, Ivory. Interview, Baltimore, Maryland, 7 Feb. 1975.
Doce, Alphonso. Interview, Bridgeport, Connecticut, 6 Aug. 1976.
Dowling, Dave. Interview, Madison, Illinois, 30 Dec. 1976.
Evett, Samuel. Interview, Calumet City, Illinois, 4 March 1976.
Frasier, Jean. Interview, Hamilton, Ontario, 4 June 1976.
Freer, John. Interview, Hammond, Indiana, 16 Nov. 1976.
Gagnon, John. Interview, Las Vegas, Nevada, 1 Sept. 1976.
Gil, Roberto. Interview, East Chicago, Indiana, 30 March

1976.
Gilks, George. Interview, Toronto, Ontario, 22 Nov. 1976.
Graczyk, Tony. Interview, Chicago, Illinois, 21 June 1977.
Green, Walter. Interview, Gary, Indiana, 23 May 1976.
Gyurko, Joe. Interview, Hammond, Indiana, 13 May 1976.
Haaf, Gary. Interview, Cheektowaga, New York, 16 Aug.
        1976.
Hopper, Mary. Interview, East Chicago, Indiana, 5 May 1976.
James, Ed. Conversations, Chicago, Illinois, 26 Sept. 1976,
        Hammond, Indiana, 8 Nov. 1976.
Jones, Ray. Interview, Sudbury, Ontario, 8 June 1976.
Julian, Dave. Interview, Houston, Texas, 27 Dec. 1976.
Kaczocha, Paul. Interviews, Gary, Indiana, 20 March 1976,
        Hammond, Indiana 5 Aug. 1977.
Kennedy, Ola. Interview, Gary, Indiana, 29 Jan. 1976.
Kimbley, George. Interviews, Gary, Indiana, 27 March 1976,
        and 11 Nov. 1976.
Kmec, Andrew. Interview, Chicago, Illinois, 25 Oct. 1976.
Kmetz, Frank. Conversation, Chicago, Illinois, 26 Sept. 1976.
Koleff, Nick. Interview, East Chicago, Indiana, 5 March
        1976.
Kotelchuck, Joseph. Interview, Baltimore, Maryland, 7 Feb.
        1975.
Kransdorf, Joseph. Interview, Chicago, Illinois, 2 Aug. 1977.
Litch, Bill. Interview, Liberty, Ohio, 30 Oct. 1976.
Lovely, Keith. Interview, Sudbury, Ontario, 7 June 1977.
Lyons, Jim. Interview, Chicago, Illinois, 2 June 1976.
Mackral, Walter. Interview, Gary, Indiana, 22 May 1976.
McGarry, William. Interview (telephone), 4 March 1982.
McMills, Michele. Interview, Homestead, Pennsylvania, 30 Jan.
        1977.
McSevney, Bob. Interview, Hamilton, Ontario, 3 June 1977.
Mancinelli, Sergio. Interview, Las Vegas, Nevada, 1 Sept.
        1976.
Mann, Ed. Interview, Hubbard, Ohio, 30 Oct. 1976.
Manzardo, Mario. Interview, Chicago, Illinois, 24 Nov. 1975.
Marshall, Scott. Interview, Birmingham, Alabama, 20 Dec.
        1976.
Massengill, Ken. Interview, Merrillville, Indiana, 7 Oct. 1976.
Mezo, Cliff ("Cowboy"). Interview, East Chicago, Indiana, 16
        April 1976.
Mills, Tom. Interview, East Chicago, Indiana, 6 May 1976.
Montgomery, Oliver. Interview, Chicago, Illinois, 25 Oct.
        1976.
Morris, Brent. Interview, Bessemer, Alabama, 20 Dec. 1976.
Morris, William R. Interview, Houston, Texas, 27 Dec. 1976.
Norrick, Joe. Interviews, Gary, Indiana, 28 Nov. 1975, 7
        Nov. 1976.
Olszanski, Mike ("Oz"). Interview. Dyer, Indiana, 11 May
        1976; conversations, Las Vegas, Nevada, 30 Aug.-3
        Sept. 1976.
Pacheco, Basil. Interview, East Chicago, Indiana, 18 Jan.
        1976.
Patterson, Dave. Interview, Sudbury, Ontario, 7 June 1977.

Patterson, George.   Interview, Evergreen Park, Illinois, 18
     Nov. 1975.
Pena, Joe.   Interview, Gary, Indiana, 1 May 1976.
Petrosky, Louis.   Interview, Gary, Indiana, 28 Feb. 1976.
Peurala, Alice.   Interview, Chicago, Illinois, 10 Aug. 1977.
Piccirilli, Paul.   Interview, Pittsburgh, Pennsylvania, 29 Jan.
     1977.
Purdue, Norm.   Interview, East Chicago, Indiana, 26 May
     1976.
Radovich, Joe.   Interview, Boardman Township, Ohio, 31 Oct.
     1976.
Raine, George.   Interview, Hamilton, Ontario, 6 June 1977.
Reber, Ray.   Interview, Hubbard, Ohio, 30 Oct. 1976.
Richards, Al.   Interview, Gary, Indiana, 28 Feb. 1976.
Riehle, Dave.   Conversation, Houston, Texas, 27 Dec. 1976.
Riley, H. Lee, Jr.   Interview, Gary, Indiana, 28 Feb. 1976.
Rivard, Jim.   Conversation, Chicago, Illinois, 19 Feb. 1977.
Robinson, Jim.   Interview, Hammond, Indiana, 10 July 1976.
Rodriguez, Ignacio ("Nash").   Interview, Chicago, Illinois, 23
     Jan. 1976.
Rospierski, Bob.   Interview, East Chicago, Indiana, 23 March
     1976.
Roy, Mike.   Interview, Las Vegas, Nevada, 30 Aug. 1976.
Sadlowski, Ed.   Conversations, 1975-1977.
Sargent, John.   Interview, Calistoga, California, 1 Sept. 1978.
Schendel, Herm.   Interview, Sudbury, Ontario, 8 June 1977.
Scott, Walter.   Interview, Baltimore, Maryland, 7 Feb. 1975.
Searcy, Walter.   Interview, Nashville, Tennessee, 18 Dec.
     1976.
Sims, Joe.   Interview, Youngstown, Ohio, 30 Oct. 1976.
Smith, Elizabeth (NAACP labor lawyer).   Interview, New York,
     New York, 28 Sept. 1973.
Southern, Frank.   Interview, Sudbury, Ontario, 9 June 1977.
Stan, Fred.   Conversation, Chicago, Illinois, 26 Sept. 1976.
Stenmark, John (staff member of the American Iron and Steel
     Institute).   Interview (telephone), 26 Feb. 1982.
Stevenson, Ray.   Interview, Toronto, Ontario, 22 Nov. 1976.
Strong, Curtis.   Interview, Gary, Indiana, 15 Feb. 1976.
Taylor, Cec.   Interviews, Hamilton, Ontario, 17 Aug. 1976,
     Toronto, Ontario, 23 Nov. 1976, Hamilton, Ontario, 7
     June 1977; conversations, 1976-1983.
Tester, Jim.   Interview, Sudbury, Ontario, 8 June 1977.
Todd, William.   Interview, Gary, Indiana, 28 Feb. 1976.
Toll, Bill.   Interview, Hamilton, Ontario, 4 June 1977.
Tomko, Tony.   Interview, Elizabeth, Pennsylvania, 30 Jan.
     1977.
Walsh, Peter.   Interview, Sudbury, Ontario, 7 June 1977.
Wellington, Al.   Interview, McDonald, Ohio, 31 July 1976.
Wilson, Dave.   Interview, Baltimore, Maryland, 7 Feb. 1975.
Wood, Carl.   Interviews, Gary, Indiana, 28 Feb. and 11 March
     1976.
Wood, Roberta.   Interview, Chicago, Illinois, 25 May 1977.
Wright, Sylvester.   Interview, Birmingham, Alabama, 22 Dec.
     1976.

Yates, Bill.   Conversation, Chicago, Illinois, 9 Jan. 1977.
Young, Bill.   Interview, Gary, Indiana, 8 April 1978.

NOTE: Unless otherwise noted, the interviewees were members of the Steelworkers Union, were members of the union staff, or were directly involved in reform activity in the union. Also, unless otherwise noted, the interviews were conducted face to face.   Although not all the interviews are directly cited in the text, the understanding of Steelworker politics and of the reform movement that was provided by all these interviews provided me with the perspective needed to write this book.

NAME INDEX

SUBJECT INDEX